Best wishes
Pemba Lama.

The Ultimate Nepalese Cook Book

Author
Pemba Lama

Project editor
Annie Watsham
griersonpublications.com

Art direction and design
Gavin Ambrose
gavinambrose.co.uk

Photography
Tony Jones
tonyjonesphotography.co.uk

Editorial and design assistant
Louise Watsham

Food styling
Gavin Ambrose & Louise Watsham

First published in Great Britain in 2012 by
griersonpublications.com

ISBN 978-0-9571541-0-0

All rights reserved. No reproduction, copy or transmission of this publication may be made without written permission. No paragraph of this publication may be reproduced, copied or transmitted save with written permission or in accordance with the provision of the Copyright Act 1956 (as amended). Any person who does any unauthrorised act in relation to this publication may be liable to criminal prosecution and civil claims for damages.

Text 2012 Grierson Publications Limited

Photography 2012 Tony Jones Photography

Front cover photograph Tony Jones

Pemba Lama is hereby identified as the author of this work in accordance with section 77 of the copyright, Designs and Patents Act 1988

Front cover: prawn curry (see page 98)

grierson
publications

The Ultimate Nepalese Cook Book

Pemba Lama

I would like to acknowledge with gratitude the help and support I have received from the following people in helping to bring about the publication of The Ultimate Nepalese Cook Book:

Annie Watsham the 'mystery woman' from Cranbrook and my Editor who not only agreed to take on the book with huge enthusiasm but who edited it superbly; Gavin Ambrose for his incredible design abilities and artistic skill in making the food look even better at the photo shoot; Tony Jones for his superb and detailed photography (and patience whilst waiting for freshly cooked dishes!); Louise Watsham, who also patiently amended recipes as we went and for her superb design and proofreading skills; Alice Dewing for her outstanding proofreading; Nicci Gurr, my co-chef, with whom I had a lot of laughs and from whom I learnt so much and to Grahame Grant – just for being there with his camera at the photo shoot and for making me laugh!

And not forgetting my ever-patient wife, Diki and daughters Kessang and Linda who understood the long hours I had to put in to cook, write, rewrite and then edit the recipes – to you all a huge thank you for making my dream come true!

Pemba Lama.

contents

introduction

Nepal is a culturally diverse nation with an equally diverse variation in the availability of culinary ingredients. Given its landlocked location, there has been an inevitably significant influence on Nepalese cuisine from its neighbouring countries India, China and Tibet and although curries are commonplace, as is for example naan bread, each dish within this book is given its own unique Nepalese twist.

The eating patterns of the Nepalese people have evolved over time. Nowadays Nepalese cooking encompasses a variety of fusions from Chinese, Tibetan and Indian cooking, resulting in authentic Himalayan cuisine. Gurkha-style food does have its own exclusive character, mainly due to the careful and exciting addition of fresh ingredients, various spices, seasonings and flavourings, many of which are exclusive to Nepalese cooking.

What I believe is unique about the art of Gurkha and Nepalese cooking is the innate understanding and careful balancing of spices and herbs as well as the introduction of oriental and tropical ingredients into its dishes, for example, coconut from Malaya to Chinese-style stir fries.

Masalas or spices are grown widely in the plain areas of Nepal and the import and export of spices with neighbouring India is a common trade, hence the names of spices are similar to those used in Indian cookery. The majority of spices used in this recipe book can now be easily found in larger supermarkets nationally and internationally and of course, most Asian grocery stores. When preparing spices you should aim to use only the quantity that will be required for the dish that is being prepared at the time, thus ensuring maximum taste and minimum wastage.

The techniques used in the creation of Nepalese recipes are reliant on the expert and subtle extraction of the variety of flavours that are encompassed within these various exciting spices and herbs. Most ingredients have more than one taste depending upon how they are used and cooked, whether they are combined with others, ground individually, used whole or fried.

In the past, all Gurkha Regiments had their own catering platoon, however as technology evolved, so did the methods of cooking, from the open wood fire to modern gas/electric cookers. However, what has remained the same in Nepalese cookery is the importance of freshly prepared herbs and spices, often using the old technique of pestle and mortar!

Food also plays a crucial part in all Nepalese festivals which are a hugely important aspect of Nepalese culture. The most important festivals are Dashain and Tihar in October and November.

Interestingly, the use of different variations of ingredients in Gurkha cooking was adapted during their permanent move to stations in India, Malaya and Brunei in the mid 1950s, then Hong Kong in the 1970s and the United Kingdom in the mid 1990s. For example the use of shellfish in their cooking – shellfish was not always a

conventionally consumed food in Nepalese cuisine. However, it became increasingly popular in Nepalese households due to the Gurkhas who served in Hong Kong, Singapore and Malaysia gaining a distinct taste for fish and shellfish dishes!

Most Gurkha soldiers, and the Nepalese people in general, are passionate about cooking. During the initial phase of Gurkha military training, the soldiers entertained themselves by singing, dancing and creating meals with their own unique style. This is commonly known as 'Gurkha Messing' – a memorable and enjoyable time to relax and forget the hardships of the rigorous Army training. This trend has been passed on for many generations and wherever the location may be, it is still a ritual practiced amongst today's young recruits.

Today great value is placed on the art of cooking in Nepal. This has seen the contemporary Gurkha Regiments giving a great deal more appreciation to their chefs, leading to a rise in demand for the very role that was once deemed an embarrassment. I, myself am very proud to be a Gurkha soldier and a Gurkha chef!

Jai Gurkha!

1

basic spices and a bit of science

The following spices and herbs are required to create the quintessential Nepalese dishes

DRY SPICE SEEDS
- Ajowan
- Bay Leaves
- Black onion seeds
- Cardamom seeds
- Cinnamon sticks
- Cloves
- Coriander seeds
- Cumin seeds
- Dry chillies
- Fenugreek seeds

POWDER SPICES
- Chilli powder
- Cumin powder
- Coriander powder
- Garam masala
- Turmeric

FRESH SPICES
- Ginger and garlic paste
- Fresh chillies
- Fresh coriander

bay leaves cardamom pods cinnamon cloves

Spices that are used in many of our favourite Nepalese dishes may also help to prevent disease and relieve pain. The characteristics and findings of such spices are as follows:

AJOWAN is called Jwano in Nepali and is a member of the Umbelliferous family, which has some 2,700 members including dill, caraway and cumin. Ajowan seeds contain an essential oil which is about 50% thymol which is a strong germicide, anti-spasmodic and fungicide. Thymol is also used in toothpaste and perfumery. It is used in a steeped liquid form against diarrhoea and flatulence.

BAY LEAVES are widely used throughout the world, best known in bouquets garnis or used similarly in soups, sauces, stews, fish, meat and poultry. The bay leaf has many properties which make it useful for treating migraine headaches, bacterial and fungal infections and gastric ulcers. Bay leaves have also been shown to help the body process insulin more efficiently, which leads to lower blood sugar levels.

CARDAMOM seeds are considered to be a strong antiseptic and antimicrobial spice by herbalists. It is also a mild aphrodisiac as well as helping to relieve flatulence.

CHILLIES are an excellent source of beta carotene and vitamin C. They help to relieve nasal congestion and prevent blood clots that can lead to a heart attack or stroke. Chillies are more nutritious than sweet peppers, with green varieties generally having a higher nutritional content than the red. They are also a very good source of antioxidants. Scientists believe that chilli contains bioflavonoids – a plant pigment that can help to prevent cancer.

CINNAMON is one of the oldest spices. Its antiseptic properties aid in killing the bacteria that causes tooth decay. The latest beneficial ingredient found in cinnamon is MHCP, a chemical that helps stimulate de-activated fat cells in patients with Type II diabetes to respond to the presence of insulin.

CLOVES are the cultivated closed flower buds of an evergreen tree grown in Indonesia. Dried, the buds have a strong aroma and, when bitten, can leave a numb sensation. This is caused by eugonol, the main component of clove oil, and makes for an instant remedy for toothache. In dentistry, mixed with zinc oxide, it has been used in root canal works as a disinfectant.

CORIANDER is rich in antioxidants and was said to be used by the Romans to help preserve meat. Though originally from North Africa, coriander can be found in some British fields and often grows by rivers. It is an anti-inflammatory and helps relieve the pain of arthritis. Its seeds and essential oils are used in preparations for indigestion. A natural bactericide, it can also prevent infection in minor wounds, while its odour-fighting compounds make it a useful ingredient in the manufacture of some deodorants.

cumin fenugreek seeds garam masala paprika

CUMIN contains phytochemicals – chemicals that are found in plants. Several phytochemicals, including those in cumin, have been found to block various hormone actions and metabolic pathways that are associated with the development of cancer and heart disease. The phytochemicals appear to work alone, as well as in combination with vitamins and other nutrients in food, to prevent cancer. The main anti-cancer agents in cumin are carevol and limonene.

FENUGREEK has been used as a food (vegetable), spice and medicine since ancient times and is commonly eaten in many parts of the world. Medicinally it has also been used for the treatment of wounds, abscesses, arthritis, bronchitis, and digestive problems such as constipation. Fenugreek has in recent times been found to be effective in the treatment of diabetes and high cholesterol.

GARLIC is a perennial bulbous plant related to the onion and is thought to be one of the world's oldest medicines. It is well known for its antiseptic and disinfectant qualities, and is said to help lower cholesterol, blood pressure and blood sugar levels and helps to purify the blood. Garlic also contains allicin, which is a potent anti-cancer agent, and it increases protection from stomach cancer by promoting the production of protective enzymes in the stomach.

GINGER is the root of the ginger plant, which is native of Asia and is used to treat a variety of conditions, from colic to rheumatism. Although it is traditionally known to improve digestion and alleviate bloating, ginger is also known to decrease motion sickness and nausea and could also act as an effective pain reliever from arthritis. The spice comes as a supplement called Zinaxin. Ginger is also a traditional cold remedy and contains the antioxidants gingerol, shagaol and zingerone. It is the zingerone that reacts with the free radicals that can cause tissue damage and joint inflammation.

NUTMEG is usually associated with sweet, spicy dishes. It mixes well with many cheeses, and is included in soufflés and cheese sauces. Used in small quantities nutmeg can reduce flatulence, aid digestion, improve the appetite and treat diarrhoea, vomiting and nausea.

TURMERIC is a member of the ginger family and grows extensively in India, China and Southern Asia. Orangey-yellow in colour, it is an essential ingredient in most curry dishes. Just a teaspoonful of turmeric can strengthen the liver and aid digestion. It is a powerful antioxidant, antibacterial and anti-inflammatory which makes it useful as an anti-cancer agent. Turmeric has also been found to help with digestion as well as guard against heart attacks and cancer of the colon.

PAPRIKA is made from dried and ground up sweet red peppers or chilli peppers and is unusually high in vitamin C. The capsicum peppers used for paprika contain six to nine times as much vitamin C as tomatoes. As an antibacterial agent and stimulant, paprika can help normalize blood pressure, improve circulation, and increase the production of saliva and stomach acids to aid digestion.

2

basic ingredients

Spices and herbs are the main ingredients in most Nepalese dishes and no kitchen would be complete without them.

As a healthy option most Nepalese households use dry spice seeds, rather than using readily available ground spices and for cooking small portions these spices are prepared fresh by grinding in a pestle and mortar.

In a typical Gurkha kitchen, oriental spices and sauces are commonly used by blending together hot spices from the Indian sub-continent and mild aromatic oriental spices from the Far East which are used either in marinating or in most stir fry dishes

The four essential requirements for Nepalese and Gurkha cooking

1 garam masala Approximately 200g

100g cumin seeds
100g coriander seeds
5 cardamom pods whole
6 cloves
20g black peppercorns
1 3cm cinnamon stick
2 white chillies (dry)
3 bay leaves

Preheat the oven to 150°C.

Pick and wash the cumin and coriander seeds in several changes of water, drain and spread onto an oven tray. Place into the heated oven and roast until crisp but without colour.

Remove from the oven and allow to cool. Mix all remaining ingredients and crush – using either an electric grinder or pestle and mortar – into a fine powder.

note

The recipe is mild-hot in taste (suitable for all types of curry dishes) and the quantities listed may be altered to produce various strengths of curry according to taste.

This masala can last up to six months in an airtight container.

2 ta-za (fresh) masala

2 dry red chillies
50g cumin seeds
50g coriander seeds
3 cardamom seeds
3 cloves
1 small cinnamon stick

Wash all ingredients separately and soak in cold water for about 30 minutes.

Mix all ingredients together, drain and crush to a smooth paste by using a stone grinder /pestle and mortar or electric blender adding a little water as necessary.

note

This freshly ground masala is suitable for any type of meat or vegetable dish in traditional Gurkha and Nepalese cooking. It is best freshly made and used as soon as possible.

3 ginger and garlic paste

250g ginger
150g garlic
100ml oil olive oil or vegetable oil

Wash, peel and rewash ginger. Slice and roughly chop. Peel the garlic by splitting into halves.

Mix the ginger and garlic, add the oil and blend by to a fine paste using either a blender or food processor.

Put into a container or bottle. This will last several weeks in the fridge as it is preserved in oil. It can also be stored in the freezer.

4 gurkha curry sauce Approximately 500ml

500g onions
100g tomatoes
2tbsp garam masala
1tsp turmeric
1tsp chilli powder
100ml vegetable oil
1 small cinnamon stick
3 cardamom seeds
1tbsp ginger and garlic paste
2 bay leaves
1tbsp tomato purée
Salt to season

Peel and roughly chop the onion, wash and roughly chop the tomatoes.

Mix the garam masala, turmeric and chilli powder in a small bowl with a little water to make a thin paste.

Heat the oil in a heavy based saucepan, fry the cinnamon and cardamom, add chopped onion and cook until golden brown in colour. Add the ginger and garlic paste and cook further 1-2 minutes stirring constantly to prevent sticking to the bottom of the pan.

Add the masala paste and bay leaves and cook for a few seconds, add tomato purée and chopped tomatoes. Simmer gently for about 30-40 minutes.

A little water may be added at this point to get the right consistency. The sauce is now ready!

3

simple starters

Commonly known as tipan tapan in Nepalese (which means titbits or tasty hot snacks) these delicious offerings are a must at every Gurkha Regiment party, buffet or dinner!

In every Nepalese household, guests are always offered these tasty hot snacks with drinks as an appetiser, followed by a delicious curry buffet.

There are many varieties of tipan tapan items in Nepalese cuisine and I've included a few here – from koftas to irresistible momos – which are simple to make and absolutely delicious to eat

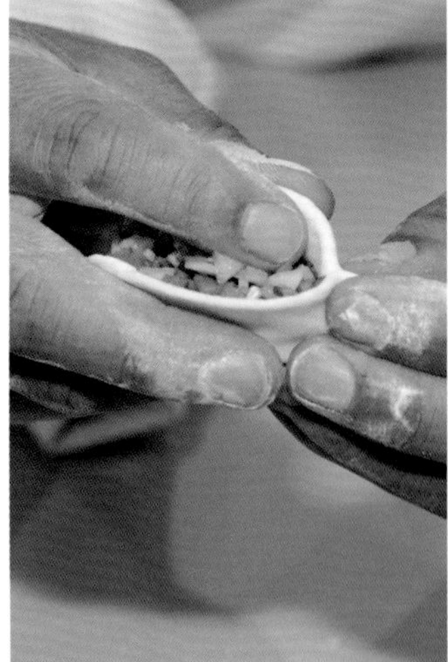

sabji momo *(vegetable)* Serves 4-6

dough
300g plain flour
175ml water, approximately

filling
200g green cabbage
100g onion, roughly chopped
20g ginger, finely chopped or juiced
2 sticks celery, peeled and chopped
50g carrots, grated
50g fresh coriander, chopped
50g spring onions, chopped
20ml light soy sauce
Pinch cumin seeds
20ml olive oil
Salt to taste

Sift the flour into a bowl, add water and make simple plain dough mix well and knead for 3-5 minutes by adding a little flour if required to achieve a stiff dough, cover to avoid drying out then allow to rest for few minutes.

Wash and finely chop the cabbage, then mix all other ingredients into a bowl with olive oil and salt.

Divide the dough into 15g balls. Roll out each ball to roughly 7cm in diameter onto a floured surface. Place a spoonful of the filling in the centre, lift and hold the pastry in one hand and pinch together by crimping, folding and pressing the edges with the aid of your thumb and forefinger to form a semi-circle.

Grease a steamer tray and place the momos onto the tray leaving space around each momo.

Repeat for the rest and steam for about 10-12 minutes.

Remove the momos carefully and serve immediately with either soup and/or chutneys (see page 108).

beef/pork momo Serves 4-6

to make dough
300g plain flour
175ml water, approximately

to make filling
250g minced beef or pork
150g onion, roughly chopped
20g ginger, finely chopped
1 stick of celery, finely chopped
50g fresh coriander, chopped
50g spring onions, chopped
20ml light soy sauce
30ml olive oil
Pinch cumin seeds
30ml boiled water
Salt to taste

Sift the flour into a bowl, add water and make a simple dough. Knead for 3-5 minutes to form a slightly harder dough then allow to rest for few minutes. Wash the meat in cold drinking water to remove excess fat, drain and set aside in a bowl. To make the filling, mix all the remaining ingredients together including the hot water and mix well.

Roll out the dough to about 3mm thickness on a lightly floured board and then cut out a 7cm circle. Repeat the process of rolling and cutting. Do not leave in the open air for too long as the pastry will dry out and easily crack.

Place 1tsp of the filling in the centre of each momo and hold it in one hand, pinch together by crimping, folding and pressing the edges with the aid of your thumb and forefinger to form a semi-circle.

Grease a steamer tray and place the momos onto the tray leaving space around each momo and steam over the boiling water for about 15-18 minutes for beef or 18-20 minutes for pork. Remove the momos carefully and serve immediately.

Best served with cooked tomato chutney (see page 111) or with blended tomato and coriander chutney (see page 113).

vegetable singara/samosa Serves 4-6

- 250g plain flour
- 1/2 tsp baking powder
- Pinch of salt
- 100g margarine
- Pinch black onion seeds
- Pinch fennel seeds
- 100ml water (approx)
- 250g boiled potatoes, fully cooked
- 30ml cooking oil
- 5g panch porang
- 100g onions, chopped
- 1tsp ginger and garlic paste (see page 21)
- Pinch turmeric, for colouring
- 1/4tsp chilli powder
- 1/4tsp black pepper
- 1tbsp garam masala (see page 20)
- Salt, to taste
- 100g peas, pre-cooked
- 10g fresh coriander, chopped
- Oil for deep frying (approximately 1ltr)

Sift the flour, baking powder and salt in a bowl; mix in the margarine and rub in the flour to create a sandy texture and add a pinch of black onion seeds and fennel seeds. Add water and gradually mix to form a medium to hard dough. Knead well for a few minutes, cover and leave to rest for 30 minutes.

Roughly chop the cooked potatoes. Heat the oil (30ml) in a pan or wok, fry off the panch porang seeds until the seeds start to burst, turn the heat to low and add the onions and ginger and garlic paste, fry until lightly coloured. Add turmeric, chilli powder, black pepper, garam masala and salt, mix the chopped potatoes and peas and stir well. Remove from heat, add chopped coriander and allow to cool.

Divide the dough into small balls and roll into very thin circles. Cut each circle in half, lift one end across the centre and moisten the edge with water. Bring another end over the moistened part to make a triangle cone, seal well.

Hold the cone in one hand opening the cavity wide. Fill the cavity three quarters full with the mixture. Moisten the top edges with water and seal well bringing one end to the other. Repeat for the rest.

Heat the oil and deep fry the samosas on a moderate heat, a few at a time, for about 5-8 minutes or until the pastry is cooked to a nice golden colour. Drain and serve warm, garnished with finely chopped red chilli and spring onions with the accompaniment of sauce, preferably hot, sweet and sour of any flavour.

'a hot, sweet and sour sauce such as tamarind sauce can be a good accompaniment to serve with samosas'

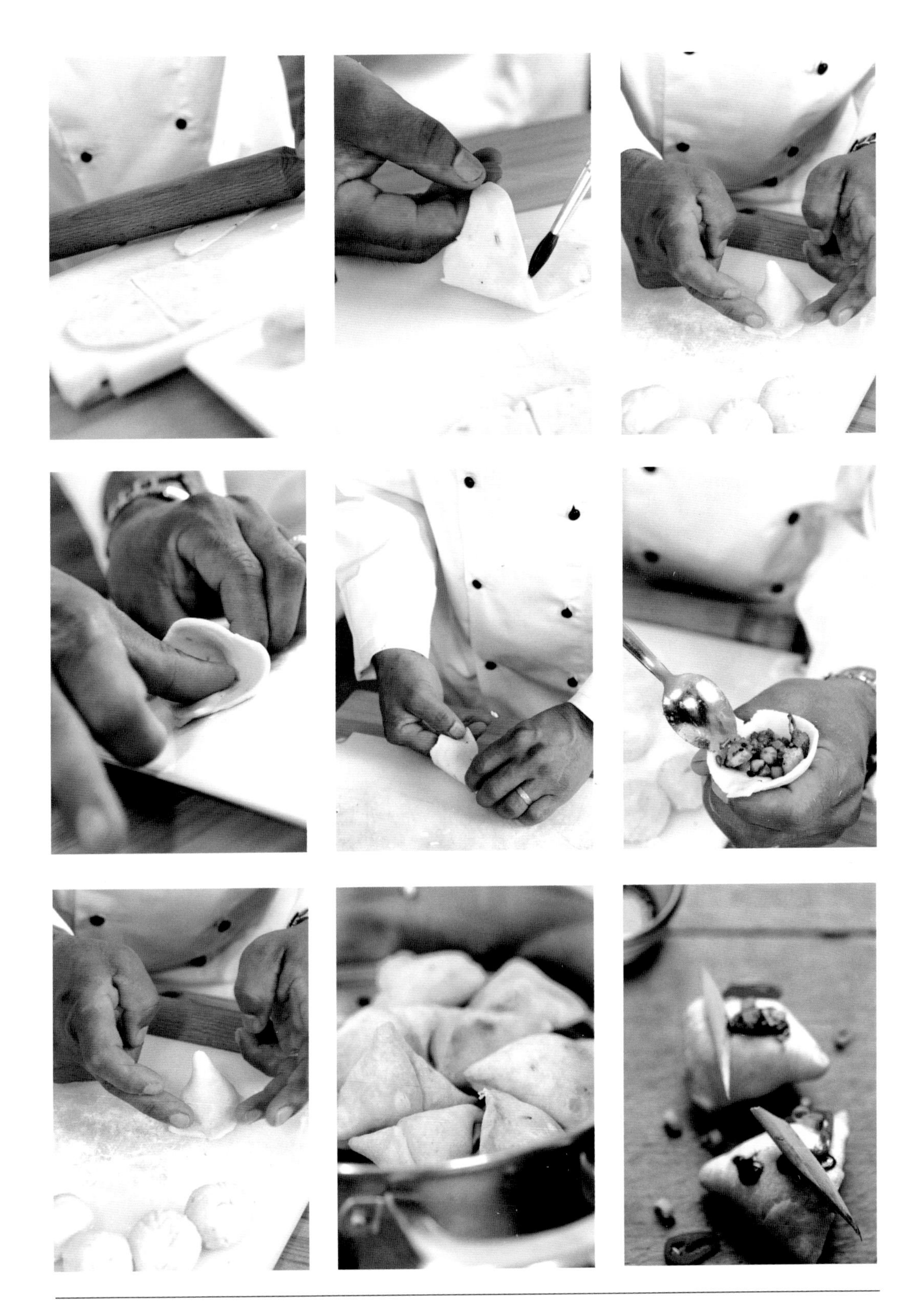

koftas *(meat balls)*

Approx 20-25 meat balls

- 1l vegetable oil for deep frying
- 1tsp cumin seeds,
- 100g onion, finely chopped
- 500g minced beef
- 1tsp ginger and garlic paste (see page 21)
- 1tbsp fresh coriander, chopped
- 1tsp turmeric
- 2 red chillies, chopped
- 50g plain flour
- 1 egg, lightly beaten
- 2tbsp soy sauce
- 1tsp garam masala (see page 20)
- 1tsp salt
- About 2l water or stock

Heat 2tbsp oil in a pan, fry the cumin seeds, add onion and sweat until without colour. Remove from heat and let it cool down, combine all ingredients; minced beef, onions, ginger and garlic paste, coriander, turmeric, chillies, flour, egg, soy sauce, garam masala and salt and put through a mincing machine or robot coupé for a quick blend. Do not overwork, otherwise it will turn wet and sticky.

Form into small balls or suitable round sizes with a little oil on your palms to avoid stickiness and then place kofta on a tray until all the mixture is used.

Boil the water or stock in a deep saucepan and blanch the koftas by dropping them in. They will sink to the bottom, and as they float up, remove, drain and set aside until all are done.

Heat the oil for deep frying to 170°C, fry a small batch of blanched koftas as required and continue to fry until golden in colour.

Remove, drain and serve with hot tomato chutney.

hot tomato chutney

2 red chillies
1tbsp coriander, chopped
$^1/_2$tsp salt
3 tomatoes

Crush the chillies and fresh coriander in a pestle and mortar with a little salt. Blanch the tomatoes, peel the skin and crush together with the chilli mixture to a rough paste and serve. Ideally use a hand blender for a quick and easy way to make this chutney.

dumba ko satay *(lamb satay)* Serves 4-6

500g boneless lamb or mutton
150g onion
100g green pepper
100g red pepper
50g mushroom button
150ml vegetable oil for shallow frying or basting, grill, if preferred

to make marinade
1tsp cumin seeds, crushed
1tsp ginger and garlic paste (see page 21)
1tbsp Tabasco chilli sauce
Juice of 1 lemon
2tbsp soy sauce
2 bay leaves
2tbsp dry sherry or rice wine
Salt to season

to make dipping sauce
1 green chilli
1 clove garlic
1tsp crushed timmur or Szechuan pepper
2tbsp light soy sauce
3tbsp olive oil
Crush the whole green chilli and garlic to a fine paste, add timmur or Szechuan pepper, soy sauce and olive oil. Mix well and serve

Dice the meat into roughly 2.5cm cubes, cut the onion and peppers to approximately the same size as the meat, halve the mushrooms or leave whole if they are small.

Once prepared, mix the meat and vegetables in a bowl and marinade with the cumin seeds, ginger and garlic paste, chilli sauce, lemon juice, soy sauce, bay leaves, dry sherry or rice wine and salt; Leave to stand in the fridge for a few minutes.

Soak some bamboo skewers in hot water for few minutes. Thread through a bamboo skewer alternately with meat and vegetables.

Grill under a pre-heated grill, basting (oiling) occasionally until meat is cooked and tender or shallow fry in oil until the meat is a light brown colour and cook for a further 5-7 minutes in the oven.

Serve with the dipping sauce.

pyazis *(onion bhajis)* 15-20 medium sized

- 300g onions
- 1tsp salt
- 25ml malt vinegar
- 2 red chillies, medium hot
- 150g besan flour (gram flour)
- 1tsp turmeric
- Pinch cumin seed
- Pinch black pepper
- 10g fresh coriander, chopped
- 10g spring onions,chopped
- 1/2 l vegetable oil for deep frying

Peel and finely shred the onions and sprinkle with salt and vinegar. De-seed the chillies and finely shred.

Sieve the besan flour and set aside.Put the rest of the ingredients, including cumin into a bowl and mix well.

Add the besan flour and mix until a soft and thick batter is formed and vegetables are completely coated.

Scoop out the mixture using either a greased tablespoon or by scooping out with your fingers and flatten the batter slightly to form a rough circle and put onto a lightly greased tray.

Heat the oil to a high temperature (170°C) and using a flat spatula or slice, lift the pyazis from the tray and slide gently into the hot oil. Fry until a light golden colour on both sides.

Remove, drain on a piece of kitchen towel and serve hot with salsa or chutney (see page 108).

alu dam *(hot spicy potatoes)* Serves 4-6

- 500g potatoes
- 30ml vegetable cooking oil
- 10g butter
- Pinch black onion seeds
- Pinch fennel seeds
- 100g onions, chopped
- 1tbsp ginger and garlic paste (see page 21)
- 1/4tsp turmeric powder
- 1tsp chilli powder
- 1tbsp tomato purée
- Salt to season
- 2tbsp ground sesame powder
- Juice 1/2 lemon

to garnish

- 2tbsp fresh chopped coriander
- 1tbsp chopped spring onions

Wash the potatoes, boil and simmer until cooked. Drain, peel and cut into suitable bite-size chunks.

Heat the oil and butter add the black onion seeds and fennel seeds and fry for few seconds. Add the chopped onions, ginger and garlic paste, turmeric and fry until a light colour is achieved.

Mix together chilli powder and tomato pureé with a little water to a thick running consistency and add to the cooked onions.

Bring to the boil, add salt, sesame powder, lemon juice and cooked potatoes, mix in most of the chopped coriander and spring onions and quickly toss. Remove from heat and serve with a touch of chopped coriander and spring onions.

to make sesame seed powder

Dry fry 2tbsp sesame seeds to a golden colour into a pan, allow to cool and roughly grind to a powder in a pestle and mortar. Do not over work other wise it may turn greasy and lumpy.

pakoras

Pakoras are small hot snacks that include meat, eggs and vegetables. They are deep fried in batter made from gram flour. Pakoras are a favourite dish suitable for small nibbles, starters and afternoon tea and every Nepalese household cooks a variety of vegetable pakoras to offer to guests as a starter. One of the best pakora dishes is aubergine – especially when served hot and crispy!

batter for pakora 10-12 portions

350g besan flour (gram flour)
1tsp salt
1tsp turmeric
1tsp chilli powder
1tsp baking powder
500ml water
50ml malt vinegar
1tbsp fresh coriander
1tbsp spring onions

Sieve the flour, salt, turmeric, chilli powder and baking powder together. Make a well and add water and vinegar, mix well to make a thick batter consistency.

Add the chopped coriander and chopped spring onions.
The batter is now ready for use for any types of vegetable pakoras.

---

egg pakora Serves 4–6

3 eggs
250ml pakora batter
1l vegetable oil for deep frying

to make seasoned flour
50g plain flour
1tsp cumin powder
1/2 tsp chilli powder
1/2 tsp salt

Put the eggs into the boiling water and boil for 12 minutes, remove and refresh in cold water to avoid dark colouration around the yolk. Remove the egg shells and cut each egg in half using thin straight thread or string by holding the egg in your palm.

Dust with the seasoned flour, dip in the prepared batter and deep fry until golden brown in colour. Remove, drain and serve warm with hot chutney.

potato pakora Serves 4-6

250g new potatoes
250ml pakora batter
1l vegetable oil for deep frying

to make seasoned flour
50g plain flour
1tsp cumin powder
1/2 tsp chilli powder
1/2 tsp salt

Boil the potatoes in their jackets. Allow to cool and cut them into quarters, dust with seasoned flour, dip in prepared batter and deep fry until golden brown in colour.

Remove, drain and serve hot.

---

chilli pakora Serves 5

3 large green or red mild hot chillies
125ml pakora batter
1l vegetable oil for deep frying

Cut the chillies in half lengthways and de-seed. Dip in the prepared batter and deep fry in hot fat until golden brown in colour.

Remove, drain and serve warm.

---

aubergine pakora serves 4-6

1 medium sized aubergine
Pinch of salt
250ml pakora batter
1l vegetable oil for deep frying

to make seasoned flour
50g plain flour
1tsp cumin powder
1/2 tsp chilli powder
Pinch salt

Wash, trim and thinly slice the aubergine, season with salt and leave to stand for a few minutes to draw the moisture out.

Make a little seasoned flour by mixing together the flour, cumin powder, chilli powder and salt.

With a piece of kitchen towel absorb any excess moisture from the aubergine, and lightly dust with the seasoned flour; dip in the batter and deep fry until golden brown in colour.

Remove, drain and serve whilst still hot otherwise it will go slightly soggy if kept longer.

4

vegetable dishes

Vegetables are an important part of daily meals in every diet. The way they are prepared and cooked in Nepalese culture incorporates a blend of spices making vegetables more tasty, healthy and nutritious.

Varieties of seasonal vegetables are used and cooked simply to retain vitamins and minerals. Most of these vegetable dishes are also suitable to serve with traditional Western roast dinners or grilled dishes

uhshineko bhat *(plain boiled rice)* Serves 6-8

500g rice
525ml water, approximately

method 1

Pick and wash the rice in several changes of water and cover with water approximately 2.5cm above the rice level (use your first finger to measure). Bring to the boil without a lid, stirring occasionally until the water starts to bubble on the surface of rice, turn the heat down to very low and allow to simmer for about 3-5 minutes with the lid on.

Remove from heat and stand for a further 5 minutes, fluff up with a fork, turn out into a suitable dish and serve.

500g rice
2l water, approximately

method 2

Pick and wash the rice in several changes of water and cover with water, bring to the boil without a lid, stirring occasionally and cook slowly until the rice is almost cooked (approximately 80% cooked). Drain completely and simmer with lid on for 3-4 minutes on a very low heat.

Turn off the heat and let it cook in its own heat for a further few minutes, fluff up with a fork, turn out into a suitable dish and serve.

bhuteko bhat *(oriental fried rice)* Serves 4-6

1kg cooked rice
100g mixed fresh or frozen vegetables
100g cooked ham
80g shrimps
Pinch of salt
3 eggs
30ml vegetable oil
50g chopped onions
10g root ginger shredded
1 red chilli, shredded
2tbsp spring onions, chopped
2tbsp light soy sauce

Cook the rice as plain boiled rice (left) and once cooked fluff up with fork and set aside.

Blanch and refresh the fresh vegetables such as peas, carrots and beans etc. If using frozen mixed vegetables, blanch first in boiling water for 1 minute, refresh in cold water and set aside.

Cut the cooked ham into small dice. Cook the shrimps in boiling salted water for a minute or until the shrimps turn pink, remove, refresh in cold water and set aside.

Break the eggs into a bowl and beat with a fork, heat a frying pan with a little oil and fry the beaten eggs in small batches to cover the pan. Remove and cut into small dice or strips.

Heat the oil in a wok, add onions and ginger and fry until soft. Add ham, shrimps, chilli, vegetables, rice and stir fry for few minutes. Add spring onion and soy sauce, fry for a further 1-2 minutes then mix with the shredded/diced eggs and serve hot.

sabji pulao *(vegetable pulao rice)* Serves 4-6

500g rice
30g ghee
30g cashew nuts
5 black peppercorns
3 cardamom seeds
1x 5cm cinnamon stick
3 cloves
Pinch fennel seeds
1tsp turmeric
1 bay leaf
500ml water, boiling
Salt to season
150g mixed vegetables, frozen
30g raisins
1tsp saffron oil

Pick and wash the rice and soak in cold water for 20 minutes and drain.

Heat the ghee and fry the cashew nuts to a light golden colour, remove, drain on kitchen paper and set aside. In the same oil add the peppercorns, cardamom, cinnamon and cloves and fry for few seconds until the seeds starts to burst. Add the fennel seeds and turmeric and immediately add the drained rice.

Stir very carefully to avoid rice breakage, add bay leaf and pour in the boiling water, season with salt and boil continuously until the water starts to bubble at rice level. At this stage most spices will float to the top and can be discarded.

Reduce the heat, add the vegetables, raisins, fried cashew nuts and simmer with lid on for 2-3 minutes. Remove from heat, drizzle with saffron oil and allow the pan to stand without stirring for a further 5 minutes.

Fluff up with fork, turn into a suitable dish and serve hot.

golbhera ko bhat *(tomato rice)* Serves 6-8

300g basmati rice
40g vegetable oil or ghee
100g onions, shredded
1tsp ginger and garlic paste (see page 24)
1tbsp garam masala
$^{1}/_{4}$tsp chilli powder
400ml tomato juice
2 bay leaves
Salt for seasoning

to garnish
Cherry tomatoes, fresh coriander

Pick and wash the rice in several changes of water and soak it for 30 minutes. Drain and keep aside.

Heat the oil or ghee in a saucepan, add the onion and cook for a minute until without colour. Add the ginger and garlic paste, garam masala, chilli powder and cook for a few seconds. Add the rice and stir gently without breaking the grain, add the tomato juice, bay leaves and salt.

Bring to the boil, stirring occasionally until almost dry or bubbling to rice level. Cover with a lid and simmer gently for about 2-3 minutes, remove from heat and allow to stand in its own heat for a further 5 minutes without disturbing. Fluff up with a fork and serve hot in a suitable dish.

dahl *(pulses)*

Dahl in Gurkha terms refers to any pulses such as lentils (red and yellow), chickpeas, mung beans, black urad (split and whole) and many more varieties. Dahl provides good nutritional value in terms of protein and carbohydrate and is a favourite of many vegetarians who eat it to ensure their daily intake of protein. Dahl can also be cooked by adding vegetables such as potatoes, aubergines or spinach.

Many varieties of dahl are available in most Asian grocery shops and each of these varieties has a distinctive taste, texture and flavour.

The more commonly used in Gurkha cuisines are:

Chana dahl: Yellow chickpeas split with the skin removed

Moong or mung: Split with or without the skin removed

Musuri dahl: Orange lentils split with the skin removed

Kalo dahl (urad): Black lentils, split, without the skin removed

sabji dahl *(with spinach)* Serves 4-6

200g dahl chana/musuri/mung
1 red chilli
20g onions
100g spinach, watercress or other leafy green vegetable
40g vegetable oil or ghee
1tsp turmeric
1tsp ginger and garlic paste (see page 21)
1tsp garam masala
1/2 tsp salt

Wash the dahl in several changes of water. Cover with enough water and bring to the boil, skimming the surface regularly to remove any scum. Simmer until fully cooked to a smooth and soft texture.

Shred the chilli and onions then keep to one side. Wash and shred the leafy green vegetables.

Heat the oil to a moderate temperature, add the onions and fry until lightly coloured then add the turmeric, ginger and garlic, chilli and garam masala. Add the leafy vegetables and cook for 1-2 minutes.

Pour the cooked dahl over, season with salt, bring to boil and adjust the consistency, which should coat the back of a spoon or be a soup like consistency.

Serve with cooked rice and bread.

curried dahl chana Serves 4-6

200g dahl chana
30ml oil
4 cardamom seeds pods
1 small cinnamon stick
1/2 tsp coriander seeds
1 medium onion, chopped
1tsp ginger and garlic paste (see page 21)
1 bay leaf
1tsp turmeric
1tsp coriander powder
1/2 tsp chilli powder
750ml water
1tsp salt
1tbsp desiccated coconut

Wash the dahl in several changes of water and soak overnight in cold water.

Heat the oil to a moderate temperature, fry off cardamom seeds, cinnamon stick and coriander seeds. Add the onion and fry to a light colour then add the ginger and garlic paste and bay leaf, cook for a short time.

Add the dahl (drained) and cook the mixture, stir occasionally. Add turmeric, coriander powder, chilli powder and mix well. Add water then bring to boil, season with salt and simmer gently until dahl is cooked.

Mix in the coconut and adjust the consistency and seasoning, discard the cardamom, bay leaf and cinnamon and serve hot, garnished with plain yogurt and a sprinkle of chopped tomato, chilli and coriander.

curried dahl musuri *(lentil)* Serves 4-6

250g dahl musuri
30ml oil/ghee
Pinch cumin seeds
20g onions, shredded
1tsp ginger and garlic paste (see page 21)
1 fresh red chilli, chopped
1tsp turmeric
1tsp garam masala
2 bay leaves
Salt, to taste

Pick and wash the dahl, just cover with water and bring to the boil, skimming any scum off the top. Simmer until the dahl is cooked; check the consistency, which should coat the back of a spoon. If required some hot water may be added to bring the desired consistency.

Heat the oil or ghee to smoky hot, quickly fry the cumin seeds, add the onions and fry to a light golden colour, add ginger and garlic paste, chilli, turmeric, garam masala and bay leaves.

Pour the cooked dahl, adjust seasoning to taste and serve garnished with chopped coriander.

stir fried broccoli with ginger Serves 4-6

250g broccoli
1tbsp ginger
1 red chilli
30ml vegetable oil
10g butter
15ml sesame oil
Salt to season

Wash and cut the broccoli into suitable sizes, blanch in boiling salted water for 2-3 minutes, then quickly refresh in cold water to retain the colour and vitamins, drain and keep aside.

Peel, slice and finely shred the ginger into thin strips, de-seed and shred the chilli.

Heat the vegetable oil in a pan, add the butter, shredded ginger and chilli and fry for a few seconds. Add the broccoli; stir fry on a high heat for 1-2 minutes, season to taste. Sprinkle with a little sesame oil and serve.

alu ra kerao *(curried potato and peas)* Serves 4-6

250g potatoes
1tsp turmeric
Salt to season
100g frozen peas
50g onions
1 red chilli
50g tomato purée
1tsp cayenne pepper
1tbsp cumin powder
50ml vegetable oil
Pinch panch porang
1tbsp ginger and garlic paste (see page 21)
50g tomatoes, diced
150ml water

Wash, peel and cut the potatoes into rough dice (15mm) and boil in water with the turmeric and salt added. Once boiled reduce the heat and simmer slowly until the potatoes are just cooked.

Blanch the frozen peas in boiling water for one minute and quickly refresh in cold water, drain and put aside. Peel and chop the onions, slice the chilli discarding the seeds.

Mix together the tomato purée, cayenne pepper and cumin powder and add a little water to make a smooth runny paste.

Heat the oil in a pan, fry the panch porang, and as the spices start to burst, add the onions, ginger and garlic paste and fry to a light colour. Add the purée mix and cook for a further 1-2 minutes. Add the tomatoes and chilli, season with salt.

Add the potatoes and peas, mix well until thoroughly heated and serve sprinkled with chopped coriander.

french beans with coconut Serves 4-6

250g French beans
30ml olive oil
Pinch mustard seeds
$^1/_2$ onion, shredded
1tsp ginger and garlic paste (see page 21)
50g desiccated coconut
1tsp cayenne pepper
Pinch black pepper
Salt
Juice of $^1/_2$ lemon

Wash, trim and slice the beans to suitable sizes and blanch in boiling salted water for 3-4 minutes. Remove and refresh in iced water. Drain and put aside.

Heat the oil in a pan; add mustard seeds then add onion and ginger and garlic paste and fry for a minute or less until without colour.

Add desiccated coconut and fry until lightly coloured, quickly add green beans and stir fry until hot and crunchy. Sprinkle with cayenne pepper, black pepper, salt and lemon juice, toss on a high heat, until thoroughly heated.

---

alu kopi *(curried potatoes and cauliflower)*

Serves 4-6

300g potatoes
250g cauliflower
1tsp turmeric
Salt
1tbsp tomato purée
$^1/_2$tsp chilli powder
150ml water
30ml ghee/oil
1tsp panch porang
1 medium onion
1 fresh red chilli
1tbsp ginger and garlic paste (see page 21)
1 tomato, chopped
1tsp cumin powder
1tsp coriander powder

Wash, peel and cut potatoes into roughly 1.5cm dice. Prepare and cut the cauliflower into medium sized florets.

Cook the potatoes in cold water with turmeric and salt, once boiled simmer until cooked. Remove with slotted spoon and keep aside. Using the same water, blanch the cauliflower until just cooked, drain and mix with the cooked potatoes.

to make tomato paste mixture

Mix together the tomato purée, chilli powder and water and set aside.

Heat the oil or ghee and fry the panch porang to a dark brown colour, add the chopped onion, chopped chilli and ginger and garlic paste, cook lightly for a few seconds. Add chopped tomato, cumin and coriander powder, and the tomato paste mixture.

Cook slowly for a couple of minutes, season with salt and add the cooked potatoes and cauliflower, gently toss until heated through. Serve sprinkled with freshly chopped coriander.

baighun tarkari *(curried aubergine)* Serves 4-6

300g aubergine
50ml vegetable oil
Pinch panch porang
I medium onion
1tsp ginger and garlic paste (see page 21)
$^{1}/_{2}$tsp turmeric powder
1tsp cumin powder
1tsp coriander powder
1tsp cayenne or chilli powder
2 medium tomatoes, chopped
1tsp tomato purée
1tsp salt
Juice of $^{1}/_{2}$ lemon

Wash and slice the aubergine into 1.5cm thick slices and cut again into batons roughly 3.5cm long, discarding the soft middle of the aubergine.

Heat the oil in a pan, fry off the panch porang seeds and add chopped onion, cook until lightly coloured, add ginger and garlic paste and cook for a further few seconds.

Add the aubergine and cook for about 3-5 minutes, add turmeric, cumin, coriander, cayenne or chilli powder and mix well.
Add tomatoes and tomato purée and stir well, reduce heat and simmer gently until the aubergine is cooked. Season with salt, a little bit of water may be added, if required.

Finish off with a touch of lemon juice, mix well and serve sprinkled with picked coriander.

stir fried spinach Serves 4-6

300g spinach
30ml mustard oil
1/4tsp panch porang
2 cloves garlic, crushed
2 dried red chillies, whole
2tbsp light soy sauce
Salt to season

Wash the spinach thoroughly and roughly shred (baby spinach can be left whole).

Heat the oil to smoky hot and fry the panch porang until the seeds become slightly dark in colour. Add chillies and crushed garlic, stir then add the spinach.

Stir fry for 2-3 minutes, season with soy sauce and salt. Drain off any excess liquid and serve immediately.

Other green leafy vegetables may also be used in lieu.

'eggs are widely used in Gurkha cookery – especially as a vegetarian substitute'

gurkha cheese omelette Serves 4

8 eggs
Salt and pepper, to taste
15g freshly chopped coriander
1 chilli, red or green, finely shredded
20ml vegetable oil
100g grated Cheddar cheese

Break 2 eggs at a time into a small bowl, season with salt, pepper, a little chopped coriander and a touch of shredded chilli, and beat well.

Heat the oil in a small omelette/frying pan, add the beaten eggs and stir continuously with a fork or spatula until the eggs are half set but still soft and moist on top.

Remove from heat and sprinkle on the grated cheese. Finish under a hot grill until cheese is a light brown colour. Fold over and keep warm.

Continue to cook the rest and serve hot with a freshly picked coriander leaf.

---

gurkha omelette curry Serves 3

200ml Gurkha curry sauce (see page 22)
6 eggs
1tbsp fresh coriander, chopped
1tbsp spring onions, chopped
1 red or green chilli, finely shredded
Salt to taste
15g butter or ghee

to garnish
3 onion rings, coriander and Gurkha curry sauce

Make some Gurkha curry sauce as per the recipe and keep aside to serve with the omelette. Break two eggs at a time into a bowl, mix with finely chopped coriander, spring onions, chilli and salt.

Heat the omelette pan, add a small knob of butter or ghee and pour on the beaten eggs. Quickly stir the mixture continuously with a fork until the eggs are nearly set but with plenty of softness still on top.

Pour some curry sauce in the centre of the omelette, gently tip the pan and overlap the omelette to form a semi circle and flick over onto a serving dish. Repeat twice more to complete 3 omelettes.

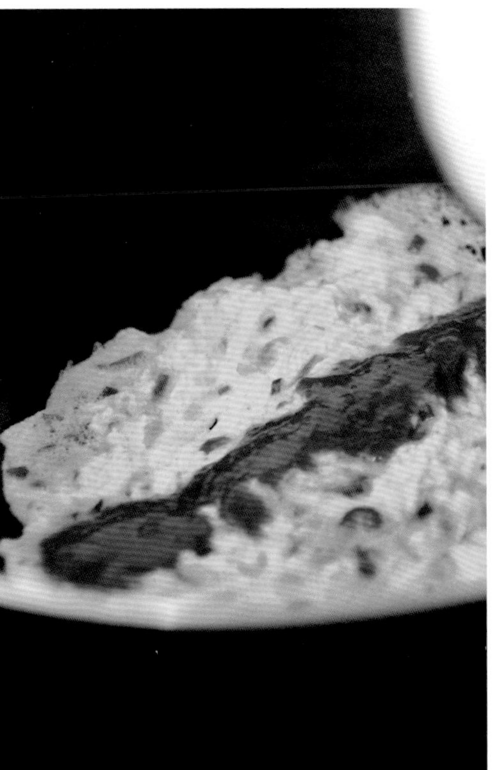

gurkha egg curry Serves 2

4 eggs
20ml vegetable oil
150ml Gurkha curry sauce (see page 22)
1/2 tsp turmeric powder
1/4 tsp cayenne pepper
Pinch of salt, to taste

to garnish
Fresh picked coriander, finely chopped chilli

Boil the eggs for 11 minutes, remove and refresh in cold water then drain and remove the shells and set aside.

Heat the oil in a small pan with a little turmeric, cayenne pepper and salt, add the peeled eggs and fry to light golden colour. Remove and put into a suitable serving dish.

Boil the prepared curry sauce, and pour lightly over the fried eggs and serve with a little garnish.

---

himalayan fried noodles Serves 4-6

200g egg noodles
1tbsp sesame oil
1 each green/red peppers
1 onion
1 each red/green chillies
2 eggs
Salt to season
60ml vegetable oil
5g ginger, shredded
1tbsp curry powder
100g cooked ham, shredded
1tbsp chopped spring onion
100g prawns
100g fresh bean sprouts
1tsp cornflour
2tbsp light soy sauce
1tsp sugar

to make cornflour solution
Mix together cornflour, soy sauce and sugar

Cook the noodles in boiling seasoned water for 3-5 minutes, stir and separate the noodles with a fork or chopsticks. Refresh in cold water, drain, drizzle with little sesame oil and set aside. Thinly slice the peppers and onion, shred the chilles, keeping all ingredients separate.

Beat the eggs in a bowl with pinch of salt and make a thin plain omelette in a frying pan with a little oil. Remove, cool and cut into thin strips and put to one side.

Heat a little oil in a shallow frying pan and fry the cooked noodles to a light golden colour and until they are crispy.

Heat a wok with a little oil, add the sliced onion and ginger and lightly cook. Add curry powder and chillies and fry for few seconds, then add ham and spring onion, and fry a further few seconds.

Add prawns, bean sprouts, peppers, stir fry for 2 minutes and thicken with cornflour solution.

Add the fried noodles and egg strips and mix well. Serve garnished with fresh coriander

5

chicken dishes

Chicken is the most commonly consumed meat throughout Nepalese culture and is therefore the must-have meat for a buffet-style Nepalese meal.

Nepalese-style chicken can be cooked in a variety of ways with blends of various spices and fresh herbs and finished off lightly coated with curry sauce (the Gurkha's favourite!). Chicken is very versatile and can also be steamed, braised, deep fried, roasted or cooked tandoori style

ahmilo peero kukhra
(hot and sour chicken) Serves 4-6

- 1 whole chicken
- 150g onion
- 1tsp ginger and garlic paste (see page 21)
- 1tbsp garam masala
- 1tsp dark mustard powder
- 1tsp black pepper
- 1tsp chilli powder
- 50ml malt vinegar
- 1tsp sugar
- Salt
- 30ml vegetable oil
- 2 tomatoes, chopped
- 1tsp tomato purée
- 2 fresh chillies
- 2tbsp fresh coriander
- 4 spring onions, chopped

Prepare the chicken by cutting into 8 -10 pieces. Peel and shred the onions.

Marinate the chicken with the ginger and garlic paste, garam masala, mustard powder, black pepper, chilli powder, vinegar, sugar and salt, cover and leave to stand in a refrigerator for about half an hour.

Heat the oil in a saucepan and cook the onions to a light colour. Then add the marinated chicken and spices mix to the pan together with the tomatoes and tomato purée, stir and simmer gently until the chicken is cooked through, a little water may be added if the chicken is too dry.

Then add the shredded chilli, chopped coriander and spring onion. Taste for seasoning, turn onto a suitable dish and serve.

Use some freshly chopped herbs to garnish the ahmilo peero kukhra.

sukmel kukhra *(chicken cardamom)*

Serves 4-6

1kg chicken breast
250g onion
280ml natural yogurt
60g cashew nuts
1tsp cardamom powder
1tsp fennel powder
1tsp cayenne pepper
1tsp turmeric
100ml vegetable cooking oil
1tbsp ginger and garlic paste (see page 21)
1tbsp cumin powder
1tbsp coriander powder
Salt to season

Cut the chicken breast into suitable sizes, peel and chop the onions.

Mix together yogurt, crushed cashew nuts, cardamom, fennel, cayenne pepper and turmeric. Blend to a fine paste in a liquidiser or blender.

Heat the oil, add the onions and fry until a light golden colour. Add ginger and garlic paste and fry until the flavour comes out. Add the chicken, cumin powder and coriander powder and cook for 3-5 minutes.

Pour over the blended mixture, reduce the heat and stir occasionally to prevent from burning the bottom of the pan. Continue to stir until chicken is cooked and tender.

Remove any excess oil and adjust seasoning, a little stock/water can be added to adjust the consistency of the sauce if required. Garnish with red chilli and fresh coriander.

bhuteko kukhra tarkari *(fried chicken curry in sauce)*

Serves 4-6

5 chicken legs
1tsp turmeric
2tsp ginger and garlic paste (see page 21)
1tsp chilli powder
2tbsp soy sauce
Salt to season
150ml vegetable oil
200g onions, chopped
1tbsp cumin powder
1tbsp coriander powder
1tsp tomato pureé
150g tomatoes
1 red chilli
2tbsp plain yogurt

Wash and cut the chicken legs into suitable pieces and marinate with 1/2 tsp turmeric, 1tsp ginger and garlic paste, 1/2 tsp chilli powder, soy sauce, salt and a little oil. Cover and leave to stand for about 30 minutes in the fridge.

Heat half the oil and shallow fry the chicken until a golden colour, remove and keep warm. Heat the remaining oil and fry the onions until light golden brown and add the remaining ginger and garlic paste, cook for a few seconds. Put the remaining ground spices (cumin, coriander, turmeric and chilli powder) into a bowl and dilute with a litre of water, add to the fried onions.

Add the tomato pureé and chopped tomatoes, stir and season with salt. Add the fried chicken and sliced chilli, cook for a further few minutes or until the chicken is cooked. Add the plain yogurt and mix well. Remove any excess oil and serve with rice or naan bread.

chicken chow mein Serves 4-6

250g chicken breast
1tsp ginger and garlic paste (see page 21)
Pinch Chinese 5 spice
1/2tsp granulated sugar
1tbsp dry sherry or rice wine
4tbsp soy sauce
2tbsp sesame oil
400g egg noodles
1 each red/green pepper
1 celery stick
1 each red/green chilli
3 spring onions
100g onions
100g mushroom
75ml vegetable oil
100g bean sprouts
1tsp cornflour
Salt and pepper to taste

Thinly shred the chicken into strips of about 5cm and marinate in the following: 1/2 tsp ginger and garlic paste, pinch of Chinese 5 spice, sugar, 1tbsp dry sherry or rice wine, 2tbsp soy sauce and 2tbsp sesame oil. Mix well and leave to stand in fridge for at least 30 minutes.

Cook the noodles in boiling water for few minutes stirring well with chopsticks to separate them. Once cooked, strain and refresh in cold water and keep aside.

Thinly slice the peppers, peel and slice the celery, de-seed and shred the chilli, slice the spring onions diagonally, slice onions and mushrooms and keep all prepared vegetables separately on a tray.

Heat a little bit of oil in a large pan or a wok to smoky hot and quickly stir fry the marinated chicken for about 1-2 minutes. Remove and keep warm.

Heat again a little oil in a wok, sauté the sliced onions, 1/2 tsp ginger and garlic paste, peppers, chilli, mushrooms, bean sprouts, celery and stir fry in high heat for 2-3 minutes. Add the cooked chicken and spring onions; thicken up with cornflour solution (see page 63).

Heat the remaining oil to smoky hot and shallow fry the cooked noodles until crispy and a light brown colour and add to the cooked vegetables in the wok. Stir well with a drizzle of sesame oil and serve immediately.

'in Gurkha cookery, Korma curry is a common dish, cooked in the centuries old traditional way by using freshly prepared masala'

kukhra ko korma tarkari *(chicken korma)*

Serves 4-6

1 whole chicken
50ml ghee or vegetable oil
300g onion, chopped
10g ginger and garlic paste (see page 21)
1tbsp cumin powder
1tbsp coriander, chopped
$^1/_2$tsp cardamom powder
$^1/_2$tsp fennel powder
2 bay leaves
10g tomato purée
150g tomatoes, chopped
1 red chilli, sliced
150ml yogurt
Salt to season

to make marinade
1tsp turmeric
1tsp chilli powder
1tsp ginger and garlic paste
1tsp cumin powder
1tsp salt
30ml vegetable oil

Prepare the chicken by cutting into 8 portions, marinate in prepared marinade and allow to stand for 1hour.

Heat the ghee or oil in a pan, add the onion and cook to a light golden colour, mix in the ginger and garlic paste, and stir well to prevent sticking at the bottom, add all the spices listed in the ingredients, including bay leaves.

Add the chicken and cook on a medium heat for 20-25 minutes. Add the tomato purée, tomatoes and sliced chilli, season to taste and cook for a further 10-15 minutes.

Add the yogurt and mix well, simmer until the chicken is cooked. Serve hot, garnish with fresh chopped coriander.

chicken and pineapple in honey sauce

Serves 4-6

500g chicken breast
Pinch of salt
1tsp ginger and garlic paste (see page 21)
Small pinch Chinese 5 spice
2tbsp light soy sauce
1 red pepper
1 fresh red chilli
1tbsp spring onion
100g tinned pineapple
2tbsp cornflour
250ml vegetable oil to deep fry or can be shallow fried if preferred

ingredients for sauce
2tbsp cornflour
2tbsp honey
200ml water
2tbsp light soy sauce
1tsp light brown sugar
1tbsp sesame oil
Pinch salt, to taste

Wash and cut the chicken diagonally into small thick strips or 2.5cm dice and mix with salt, ginger and garlic paste, Chinese 5 spice and light soy sauce, stand for a few minutes.

Remove seeds from red pepper and cut into strips roughly same size as chicken. Deseed chilli and slice thinly. Cut the spring onion diagonally. Drain tinned pineapple and cut into rough dice.

Lightly coat the chicken with cornflour and deep fry until golden brown. Remove from oil and drain on absorbent paper. Keep hot in a pre-heated oven, 160°C, for 20 minutes.

to make sauce

Mix cornflour, honey, water, soy sauce, sugar and sesame oil in a pan, bring to boil stirring constantly until sauce thickens, adjust the seasoning with a pinch of salt.

Heat 2tbsp of oil in a saucepan. Add pineapple, red peppers, chilli and chicken and toss the mixture over a high heat until chicken is heated through.

Add the sauce and mix well, add spring onion and toss for a further minute and serve garnished with freshly chopped coriander.

6

meat dishes

All types of meats are consumed in Nepalese households except in some orthodox Hindu families where beef and pork are strictly not eaten.

Pork has always been popular, however mutton or goat (and buffalo) are also eaten, but not so frequently and if it is eaten it's preferred on the bone

fried noodles with shredded pork Serves 4-6

200g pork
$^1/_2$tsp granulated sugar
Salt and black pepper to taste
4tbsp soy sauce
1tbsp dry sherry or rice wine
1tsp ginger and garlic paste (see page 21)
Pinch Chinese 5 spice
2tsp cornflour
400g egg noodles
75ml vegetable oil
50g onions sliced
1 red chilli red,sliced
80g bean sprouts
100g celery, thinly shredded
15g spring onions chopped
1tbsp sesame oil

Thinly shred the pork, cut roughly into 5cm lengths and marinate with the sugar, salt, pepper, soy sauce, sherry or rice wine, ginger and garlic paste, Chinese 5 spice and 1tsp cornflour. Mix well and leave to stand in fridge for at least 30 minutes.

Cook the noodles in boiling water for a few minutes stirring well with chopsticks to separate them. Once cooked, strain and refresh in cold water, drain and drizzle with a little vegetable oil and keep aside.

Heat half the oil into a large pan or a wok until smoky hot and quick stir fry the marinated pork for about 1-2 minutes. Remove and keep warm.

Heat the remaining oil in a pan, add the onions and cook until a light colour, add the chilli, bean sprouts and celery and spring onions and stir fry on a high heat for 1-2 minutes. Add the cooked pork, mix well, remove and keep aside.

Clean and heat the same pan/wok with some oil to smoky hot, add the noodles and stir fry until the noodles are heated through. Add the cooked pork and vegetables. Toss on a high heat, sprinkle with soy sauce and sesame oil and serve hot.

note

Beef or chicken can be used instead of pork and other vegetables such as peppers and carrots can be added as a healthy eating option.

sauté pork with celery Serves 4-6

350g boneless pork chops
200g celery
1 medium onion
1 fresh red chilli
3 spring onions
Fresh coriander
30ml vegetable oil
2tbsp chopped ginger

cornflour solution
1tbsp cornflour
4tbsp soy sauce
$^1/_4$tsp white sugar
2tbsp water

to make marinade
1tsp ginger and garlic paste (see page 21)
1tsp white sugar
2tbsp dry sherry or rice wine
1tbsp dark soy sauce
Pinch Chinese 5 spice
25ml vegetable oil
Pinch of salt

Thinly slice the pork, put into a bowl with the marinade and leave to stand for 30 minutes in the fridge.

Wash, peel and cut the celery diagonally into slices, peel and slice the onion, de-seed and roughly slice the chilli.

Roughly chop the spring onion and coriander.

Heat a little oil in a frying pan or wok to a smoky heat and quickly stir fry the pork in small batches, remove and keep hot.

Heat the remaining oil in a pan, add sliced onions, ginger, chilli and celery and cook for a further 2-3 minutes.

Add the cooked meat, half the chopped spring onion and coriander, toss on a high heat and slightly moisten with the cornflour solution, adding slowly until a good thick consistency is achieved. Serve hot and garnish with fresh coriander.

'sauté pork is one of my favourite stir fry dishes to cook! It is best cooked in small portions over a high heat and served immediately'

sweet and sour pork Serves 4-6

600g pork loin
2tbsp rice wine
Salt to season
1tsp ginger and garlic paste (see page 21)
$^1/_2$ tsp chilli powder
1tbsp light soy sauce
300g cornflour
$^1/_2$ l vegetable oil for deep frying
100g onion, roughly diced
2 green peppers diced
1 red chilli, de-seeded and sliced
2 pineapple rings, roughly diced
2 cloves garlic, crushed

Cut the pork loin into bite size pieces and marinate in the mix of rice wine, salt, ginger and garlic paste, chilli powder and light soy sauce for about 30 minutes.

Make the sweet and sour sauce as per the recipe below.

Coat the marinated pork in the cornflour and put on a dry tray to avoid the pieces sticking together. Deep fry the pork pieces until a light golden brown colour.

Remove, and keep hot in the oven at 170°C for 10-15 minutes.

Heat a pan or wok with 2tbsp vegetable oil, and then fry the onion, peppers, chilli, pineapple and garlic for about 2-3 minutes. Add the fried pork; lightly cover with the sweet and sour sauce.

Stir well until the meat is thoroughly heated. Serve hot and garnish with chopped spring onions.

'sweet and sour is traditionally thought of as Chinese but in Nepalese cuisine we produce this dish with our own slight twist using chilli as one of the main ingredients!'

sweet and sour sauce

350ml malt vinegar
100g brown sugar
100g tomato ketchup
50ml Worcestershire sauce
Salt to taste

Put the vinegar and sugar in a saucepan, bring to boil and simmer gently. Add tomato ketchup, Worcestershire sauce and salt and simmer for 30 minutes. The sauce is ready for use.

bhuteko banghur *(fried pork curry)*

Serves 4-6

1kg boneless pork
100g tomatoes
150g onion
2 fresh chillies
50ml vegetable cooking oil
5 cardamom seeds
5 cloves
1 x 2.5cm cinnamon stick
1tsp turmeric
1tsp salt
1tsp ginger and garlic paste (see page 21)
1tbsp garam masala
1tsp chilli powder
2 bay leaves
1tbsp tomato purée
1tbsp dark soy sauce
Juice of 1/2 lemon

Cut the meat into roughly 2.5cm dice. Wash and roughly chop the tomatoes, peel and slice the onions, roughly slice the chillies.

Heat the pan with a little oil and fry off cardamom seeds, cloves and cinnamon. Add the meat, turmeric and salt and cook for approximately 20-30 minutes.

Add the sliced onions and cook for 3-5 minutes, add ginger and garlic paste, cook further 1-2 minutes.

Add the garam masala, chilli powder and the remaining ingredients, cook for a further 5-10 minutes or until the meat is cooked and tender. Taste the seasoning and serve hot sprinkled with chopped coriander.

Pork can also be prepared with bone and fat if desired. Fat and meat can be left intact and sliced into roughly 5cm pieces. Fat should always be fried longer in a moderate heat and any excess fat must be removed before adding the remaining lean meat.

---

khasi tarkari *(mutton curry with sauce)*

Serves 4-6

1kg mutton or lamb, boneless
1tsp ginger and garlic paste (see page 21)
1tsp chilli powder
1tbsp curry powder
1tsp turmeric
1tsp salt
100ml vegetable oil
150ml Gurkha curry sauce (see page 22)
1 red chilli, finely shredded
Chopped fresh coriander

Wash, trim and cut the mutton into roughly 2.5cm cubes and marinate with the ginger and garlic paste, chilli powder, curry powder, turmeric, salt and a little oil. Cover and stand in the fridge for a few minutes or until required.

Make Gurkha curry sauce as per recipe. Heat the oil in a pan to a smoky heat and shallow fry the meat in small batches to quickly seal off. Remove with a slotted spoon and put into the sauce.

Bring the sauce to a boil, add water to the sauce if necessary, reduce the heat, add chilli and half the coriander and simmer gently until the meat is cooked. Serve sprinkled with remaining chopped coriander.

sherpa lamb curry Serves 4-6

1kg boneless mutton or lamb
250g potatoes
100g onion
100ml vegetable oil
2 bay leaves
1tbsp ginger and garlic paste (see page 21)
1tbsp curry powder
1tsp chilli powder
1tsp turmeric
20g tomato purée
1tbsp paprika
250ml chicken stock
150ml Gurkha curry sauce (see page 22)
2 red chillies
1tbsp fresh coriander
Salt

Cut the lamb or mutton into roughly 2.5cm cubes. Wash, peel and roughly dice the potatoes into 2.5cm cubes and dice the onion. Heat the oil in a saucepan with onion, bay leaves, ginger and garlic paste and cook until lightly coloured.

Add the curry powder and chilli powder and mix well then add the meat, sprinkle on the turmeric and cook for about 5-6 minutes, stirring occasionally.

Add the potatoes, tomato purée and paprika, mix well then add the stock and cook for about 25-30 minutes, over a gentle heat.

Add the curry paste, chillies (split in halves with seeds intact) and half the coriander and simmer gently until the meat is cooked and tender. Adjust the sauce consistency and seasoning. Boiling water can be used to adjust the final consistency of the sauce.

Best served with ting momo bread (see page 129).

masu ra shibi
(stir fried beef with french beans) Serves 4-6

300g beef fillet
80g onion
300g French beans
50ml vegetable oil
Pinch of cumin seeds
50ml stock, beef or chicken
3 spring onions, chopped
$^{1}/_{2}$tsp salt
2tbsp oyster sauce
$^{1}/_{4}$tsp crushed timmur

to make marinade
$^{1}/_{2}$tsp ginger and garlic paste (see page 21)
$^{1}/_{2}$tsp white sugar
1tsp cornflour
Pinch Chinese 5 spice powder
3tbsp soy sauce
Pinch salt

to make cornflour solution
1tsp cornflour
$^{1}/_{2}$ tsp sugar
3tbsp soy sauce

Trim all fat and sinew from the beef fillet and cut into fine slices roughly 2.5cm long.

Marinate the meat and leave to stand in fridge for 30 minutes.

Peel and roughly dice the onions and cut the beans diagonally into 2.5cm lengths.

Heat the pan or wok with half the oil and add pinch of cumin seeds. Add the marinated beef and shallow fry on a high heat for 2-3 minutes. Remove and keep warm.

Heat the wok with the remaining vegetable oil then add onions and beans and stir fry for about 3-5 minutes, moisten with stock.

Add the spring onions to the cooked beef and thicken with the cornflour solution, season to taste. Add oyster sauce, and serve sprinkled with the crushed timmur.

'a popular dish within the Nepalese community; usually served with naan or chapatti bread but also goes perfectly with rice. Potatoes in this dish are optional'

keema *(mince meat)* curry with peas and potatoes

Serves 4-6

500g lean minced beef
1tbsp cumin seeds
1tbsp coriander seeds
2 red chillies
3 cardamom seeds
1 small cinnamon stick
100g onion
200g potatoes, optional
100g green peas, frozen
2tbsp vegetable oil
1tsp ginger and garlic paste (see page 21)
1tsp turmeric
2 bay leaves
1 tbsp tomato purée
2 tomatoes, chopped
Salt to taste
1tbsp dark soy sauce

Wash the minced beef and drain. Crush the cumin seeds, coriander seeds, one chilli, cardamom and cinnamon together in a pestle and mortar.

Peel and roughly chop the onions, wash, peel and cut the potatoes into 20mm cubes. Roughly slice the remaining chilli, blanch the peas in boiling water for a minute and refresh in cold water then drain and keep aside.

Heat a little oil in a suitable pan, add the chopped onions, ginger and garlic paste, stir and cook for 1-2 minutes until lightly coloured. Add the crushed spices, minced beef, potatoes and turmeric, and cook for 4-5 minutes stirring continuously.

Add the bay leaves, tomato purée, tomatoes, chilli, salt, soy sauce and cook for a few minutes or until the potatoes are cooked and meat is tender. Adjust the consistency by adding some water or stock to make a good sauce. Add the pre-cooked peas, stir well with the meat and serve garnished with chopped coriander.

Keema curry is best served with chapattis, rotis or rice dishes.

7

fish dishes

Shellfish has not always been a conventionally consumed food in Nepalese cuisine. However, eating shellfish and fish is becoming increasingly popular in Nepalese households due to the Gurkhas who served in Hong Kong, Singapore and Malaysia gaining a distinct taste for fish and shellfish dishes.

Most fish or shellfish are commonly cooked using freshly prepared masala with an addition of fresh herbs and chillies. Gurkha style fish curry is so delicious, full of flavour as well as healthy! Fried fish is also favoured in Nepalese cooking as it tastes fresh and flavoursome when served with a rocket salad as a starter

prawn curry Serves 4-6

350g prawns, peeled
1tbsp cumin seeds
1tbsp coriander seeds
1tsp fennel seeds
2 green chillies
2tbsp fresh coriander, chopped
50ml vegetable oil
150g onions chopped
1tsp ginger and garlic paste (see page 21)
100g tomatoes, chopped
1tsp tomato purée
100ml coconut milk
150ml water
1 bay leaf
Salt to season

to make marinade
Juice of $^1/_2$ lime
1tsp curry powder
1tsp ginger and garlic paste
1tbs soy sauce

Marinate the prepared prawns with the lime juice, curry powder, ginger and garlic paste and soy sauce. Leave to stand for about 30 minutes in the fridge.

Roughly crush the cumin, coriander and fennel seeds in a pestle and mortar. Add the whole green chillies, half the fresh coriander leaves, and continue to crush to form a paste by adding few drops of water (20-30ml).

Heat the oil; add the onions and fry until light in colour, add ginger and garlic paste and crushed spices, cook for 2-3 minutes. Add tomatoes and tomato purée and cook for a further few minutes.

Add the coconut milk, water and bay leaf and simmer for about 10 minutes.

Add the marinated prawns and cook for 3-5 minutes or until the prawns are cooked, mix in the remaining chopped coriander, taste and season. Garnish with chopped coriander and serve.

hot spicy grilled sea bass Serves 2

2 fillets of sea bass
1tbsp cumin seeds
2 dry red chillies
Pinch salt
Juice of $^1/_2$ lemon
20g flour
30ml vegetable oil

to garnish
Coriander leaves, sliced lemon or chopped chilli

Prepare the fish by washing and descaling and separate into 2 long fillets, trim and cut each fillet in half to make 4 small pieces.

Roughly crush the cumin seeds, chillies and salt and use half the spice for rubbing over the fish inside and out, together with lemon juice.

Combine the flour with the remaining crushed cumin seeds, chillies and salt. Coat the sea bass with the seasoned flour and arrange over a lightly greased tray, drizzle some oil on top.

Put under a pre-heated grill, basting from time to time with oil to avoid burning and becoming dry, turn over half way and continue to grill until the fish is cooked: approximately 2-3 minutes each side under the grill or they can also be pan fried over a medium heat.

Serve hot with golbhera ko bhat (tomato rice) (see page 46).

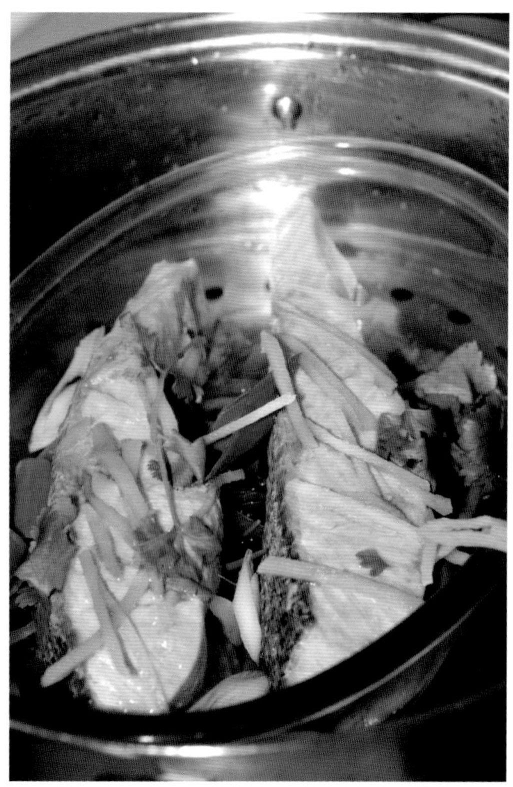

steamed fish Serves 3

3 x 130g salmon fillets
Salt to season
20g spring onions
20g coriander leaves
50g onion
1 clove garlic
1 red chilli
60ml vegetable oil
15g ginger
60ml soy sauce
Juice of $^1/_2$ lemon

to serve
boiled or fried rice (see pages 44-45)

Remove any excess scales, wash, dry and season the salmon with salt. Wash the spring onions and coriander and cut into roughly 2.5cm long strips. Peel and slice the onion and garlic, shred the chilli and keep all ingredients separate.

Arrange the fish in a suitable dish with the sliced onions underneath, sprinkle with a little salt and drizzle with a little oil, peel and cut the ginger into julienne (thin strips) and sprinkle over the fish.

Sprinkle a little soy sauce and lemon juice over the fish and steam for about 6-8 minutes then remove and arrange the spring onion, shredded chilli and coriander around the fish and steam for a further 2 minutes or until the fish is cooked.

Heat the remaining oil and fry the sliced garlic to a light golden brown colour then pour the mix over the fish with the remaining soy sauce and serve.

gurkha style fish curry

Serves 4-6

- 500g cod fillets
- 1tsp turmeric
- $^{1}/_{2}$ tsp chilli powder
- 3tbsp fresh garam masala (see page 20)
- 1tsp salt
- Juice of 2 lemons
- 100g flour
- 150ml mustard oil
- 1tsp fenugreek seeds
- 200g onion, chopped
- 1tbsp ginger and garlic paste (see page 21)
- 100g tomatoes, chopped
- 1tbsp tomato purée
- 2 green chillies, deseeded and chopped
- 250ml water
- 2tbsp sesame powder
- 2tbsp chopped coriander

Cut the cod fillets into small steaks, roughly 5cm long and marinate in 1tsp turmeric, the chilli powder, 1 tbsp garam masala, salt, juice of 1 lemon and leave to stand for 30 minutes.

Season the flour by mixing with some salt and set aside. Heat some of the oil in a frying pan, lightly coat the fish in seasoned flour and fry until pale yellow. Remove and set aside.

Heat the remaining oil in a saucepan and fry the fenugreek seeds until a dark brown colour, add onion and cook to a light golden colour. Add the ginger and garlic paste and remaining garam masala, cook for 1-2 minutes over a slow heat, then add tomatoes, tomato purée, chillies and gently cook for a further 2-3 minutes.

Add water and simmer for 10 minutes, mix the sesame powder, chopped coriander and remaining lemon juice into the sauce.

Adjust the consistency and seasoning of the sauce, add the cooked fish and cook uncovered over a medium heat for 2-3 minutes and serve with chopped coriander.

sukka bhuteko machha with salsa...
(dry fish curried) Serves 3

to cook fish and sauce
- 3 x 130g salmon pieces
- 150ml vegetable oil
- 60g onion, chopped
- 1tsp ginger and garlic paste (see page 21)
- 1tbsp fresh masala (see page 20)
- 60g tomatoes, diced
- 1tsp mustard powder
- 1tbsp sesame powder
- 2 red chillies, chopped
- Juice of 1 lemon
- 250ml water
- Salt to season
- 2tbsp chopped coriander

for salsa see page 114

to make marinade
- 1tbsp fresh masala
- 1tsp ginger and garlic paste
- Juice of 1/2 lemon
- 30ml olive oil
- Turmeric for colouring
- Salt

to garnish
- Fresh coriander, chopped and lemon slices

Clean the salmon thoroughly, put into the prepared marinade and leave to stand for 30 minutes.

Heat the oil (30ml) in a pan and cook the onion until golden in colour. Add ginger and garlic paste, fresh masala and stir for 2-3 minutes. Add tomatoes, mustard powder, sesame powder, chillies, lemon juice and cook for about 2-3 minutes. Add water, season with salt, mix in the coriander and simmer for 10-12 minutes.

Heat the remaining oil in another frying pan and shallow fry the marinated fish to a golden brown colour on both sides, turning only once. Remove, drain and keep warm in the oven.

Check the seasoning in the sauce, which should be a slightly thin consistency, add the fried fish, cook for 2-3 minutes in the sauce and serve hot.

…or with sauce

8

chutneys and sauces

Chutneys and sauces (rayatas) are served as an accompaniment to most Gurkha and Nepalese meals. Chutneys are made by the blending and cooking of chillies and tomatoes with fresh herbs for flavour.

Rayatas are completely the opposite to chutneys and are suitable for vegetarians and all ages as they are full of nutrition and can be served as a cold salad dish. Most rayatas are made by binding together vegetables (eg cucumber, carrots, potatoes, cabbage) and yogurt with lightly flavoured spices

cooked tomato chutney Serves 4-6

250g tomatoes
1 clove garlic
1tsp ginger powder
1tsp chilli powder
Salt to season
60g light brown sugar
70ml malt vinegar
20g raisins or sultanas
1tbsp honey

Wash, remove core and blanch the tomatoes in boiling water then refresh in cold ice water, remove the skin and cut into quarters. Finely chop and crush the garlic.

Put the tomatoes into a saucepan and add garlic, ginger powder, chilli and salt and cook slowly until the tomatoes are pulpy.

Add the sugar, malt vinegar, raisins or sultanas and simmer until the mixture is reduced and thickened. Add honey, mix well and serve or preserve in a bottle.

Suitable as an accompaniment to any type of dish, also ideal for sandwich fillings!

---

onion and tomato salsa Serves 4-6

100g tomatoes
80g red onions
1 clove garlic
1tsp fresh ginger
1 green chilli
1/2 tsp chilli powder
1tbsp fresh coriander, chopped
Salt
Juice of 1/2 lemon
30g Cheddar cheese, grated

Blanch and skin the tomatoes and cut into quarters, remove the inside bits (seeds and liquid) and cut into small dice. Peel and finely chop the onions, ginger and garlic.

De-seed and finely chop the chilli.

Mix together the onions, tomatoes, garlic, ginger, chilli, chilli powder, coriander, salt, lemon juice and chill for 30 minutes.

Remove any excess liquid, add grated cheese, mix well and serve.

coriander and tomato chutney Serves 4-6

200g tomatoes
2 hot red chillies
1 clove garlic
2tbsp chopped fresh coriander
Juice 1/2 lemon
1/2 tsp salt to season

Wash, remove the core and roughly cut the tomatoes. De-seed and roughly cut the chillies, peel and chop the garlic. Combine all the ingredients into a deep bowl and blend for few seconds using a hand blender.

Chill before serving.

tamarind sauce Serves 4-6

4tbsp tamarind paste (concentrated)
1tbsp sugar
2tbsp mango chutney
1tsp chilli powder
1tsp cornflour
150ml water
Salt to season

Mix all ingredients into a saucepan, bring it to boil, stir well and simmer gently for 10-15 minutes.

yogurt dip/sauce Serves 4-6

280ml plain yogurt
1tbsp granulated sugar
1/2 tsp chilli powder
1tsp cumin powder
1tbsp fresh mint, chopped

Mix all ingredients, blend to a pouring consistency and serve with aludam (hot spicy potatoes) (see page 39).

sesame flavoured hot salsa Serves 4-6

200g tomatoes
100g onions
1 clove garlic
1tsp fresh coriander
1 fresh red chilli
Salt to taste
1tbsp sesame seeds
Juice 1/2 lemon

Blanch and cut the tomatoes into small dice. Peel and finely chop the onions, garlic and coriander. Remove the seeds from the chilli and finely shred.

Mix together, the tomatoes, chilli, coriander, onions, garlic, salt and chill in the fridge for 30 minutes.

Dry fry the sesame seeds in a pan to a light golden colour. Cool and roughly crush using a pestle and mortar for few seconds. Over crushing may cause a lumpy and greasy result.

Remove chilled salsa from the fridge, squeeze in the lemon juice, fold in the sesame powder and serve.

Best served sukka bhuteko machha (see page 106).

cucumber rayata Serves 4-6

300g cucumber
Salt
1 red chilli
50g carrots
50g red onions, finely shredded
350ml yogurt
15ml mustard oil
Pinch black onion seeds

Peel and grate the cucumber, sprinkle with salt and allow a few minutes to draw out moisture then squeeze to remove excess liquid.

Deseed and finely shred the chilli, wash, peel and grate the carrots. Mix together the chilli, cucumber, onions and yogurt with a fork and let chill.

Heat the mustard oil, fry the onion seeds then remove from the heat. Arrange the chilled rayata on a suitable dish, pour over the fried onion seed and serve garnished with a touch of freshly picked coriander.

---

potato rayata Serves 4-6

600g potatoes
1 red chilli
1tbsp chopped coriander
1tbsp chopped spring onion
1/2tsp cumin powder
1/2tsp dark mustard powder
Pinch cardamom powder
Salt, to taste
350ml yogurt

Boil the potatoes in their jackets, allow to cool, remove the skins then cut into 1cm dice.

De-seed the chilli and shred finely (half mixed in and half for garnish).

Combine all ingredients into a bowl season with salt and mix well. Pour the yogurt over and carefully bind the ingredients together, and serve sprinkled with a touch of chopped spring onions, coriander and shredded chilli.

---

cabbage rayata Serves 4-6

250g white cabbage
15ml mustard oil
1/2tsp fenugreek seeds
1/2tsp black onion seeds
2 green chillies
50g red onions, finely shredded
1tbsp chopped coriander
350ml plain yogurt
Salt

Remove stalks from the cabbage and finely shred. Soak in cold salted water for 2 minutes and drain.

Heat the oil and fry the fenugreek seeds until a dark brown colour, add onion seeds and remove from heat.

Mix together the cabbage, chilli (deeseeded and finely shredded), onions, half coriander and yogurt, pour over the fried spices and serve chilled garnished with chopped coriander.

tomato and garlic chutney Serves 4-6

4 medium size tomatoes
4 cloves garlic
3 hot red chillies
Salt to taste

Wash, remove core and grill/roast the tomatoes. Remove the skin and put into a bowl. Peel and roughly chop the garlic.

De-seed and roughly chop the chillies. Combine all the ingredients using a hand blender for few seconds only. Serve.

Suitable as an accompaniment for dishes such as curry, roasts, grilled food and BBQ.

---

mixed relish Serves 4-6

100g tomatoes
100g onions
1tsp ginger
1tsp spring onions
1tsp fresh coriander
50g cucumber
50g radish
1 each red/green chillies
Salt
Squeeze of lemon juice
1tbsp sesame seeds for powder

Blanch and cut the tomatoes into small dice. Peel and finely chop the onions, ginger, spring onions and coriander.

Wash, peel and rewash cucumber and radish. Slice and finely chop the cucumber and radish. De-seed and finely shred the chillies.

Mix together tomatoes, onions, ginger, spring onions, coriander, cucumber, radish, chillies and salt and chill for 30 minutes. Remove any excess moisture, add a squeeze of lemon juice, mix in the sesame powder and serve.

to prepare sesame powder

Dry fry the sesame seeds to a golden brown then crush or grind to a rough powder.

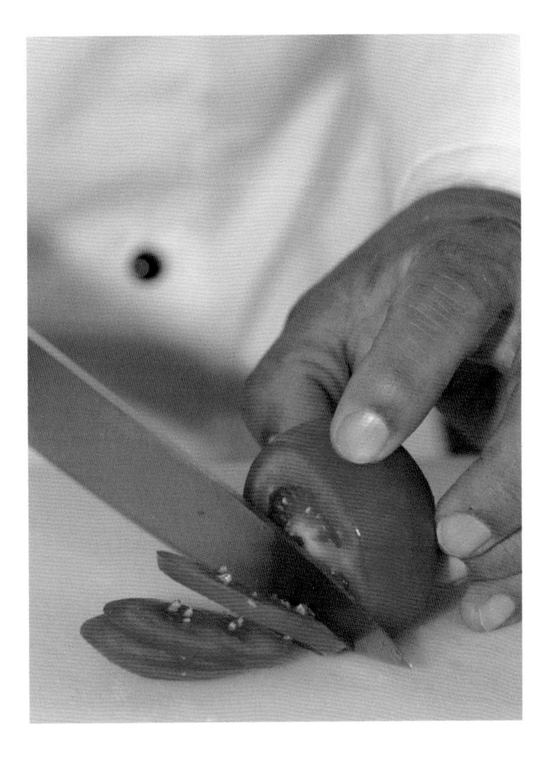

9

breads

Breads are prepared and cooked in many different ways in Gurkha and Nepalese cuisine and are an essential accompaniment to almost every dish. Not only is bread a healthy part of the diet, it is also extremely easy to cook. Dry fried chapatti or sukka roti are the most frequently consumed breads in the Nepalese household.

Naan breads, puri, paratha and pancakes are other types of breads that can be served depending on the type of meal and time of the day. Most commonly served is puri for breakfast and parathas for an afternoon snack

naan bread with fresh herbs Serves 4-6

500g strong flour
$^1/_2$tsp baking powder
Pinch salt
1tsp dry yeast
10g white sugar
225ml tepid milk
50ml natural yogurt
2 eggs
20g vegetable oil or ghee
2 cloves garlic, crushed
10g coriander, chopped

Sift the flour, baking powder and salt into a bowl; make a well, add the yeast, sugar and milk and let it ferment for 2-3 minutes. Add yogurt, eggs and oil and mix. Knead to soft and smooth dough.

Cover with a touch of oil and let it rest in a warm area until it doubles in size, then use immediately.

Knock back the dough to release the trapped air, and then divide into small balls. Roll each ball into a tear drop shape and prick with a fork, spread over some crushed garlic paste and chopped coriander and roll again a little bit to reshape. Lift the naan and pull one end to form an oval shape.

Heat up a baking tray under a grill and place the naan on the very hot baking tray, check the colour of the bread then turn over and cook both sides to a light golden colour.

Remove and keep warm under a tea towel or greaseproof paper and repeat until all the dough is finished. Serve with curry.

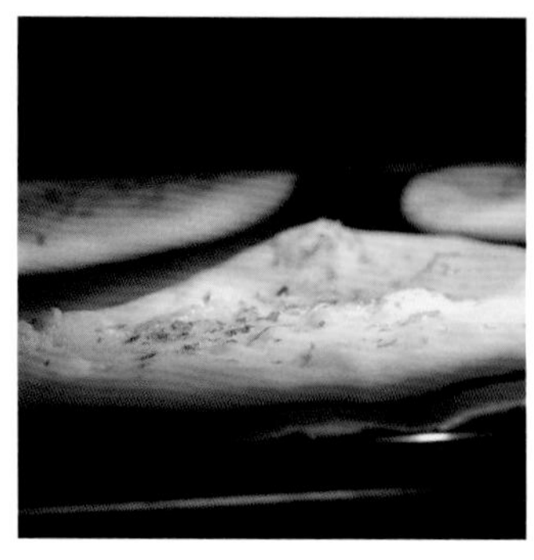

plain paratha Serves 4-6

- 500g Atta flour or plain flour
- Pinch salt
- 100g butter, cut into cubes
- 200ml water (approximately)
- 60ml olive oil
- 50ml olive oil

Sift together the flour and salt in a bowl, add the butter and rub between the fingers to a sandy texture. Make a well in the centre and add the water and mix to firm dough.

Knead the dough on a lightly floured surface until it is smooth and elastic. Place the dough into a clean bowl, cover with a damp cloth and allow to rest for half an hour.

Divide the dough into 60g balls. Roll out each piece on a greased surface into a thin circle.

Brush the top side with oil, fold in half; brush again and fold into quarter to make a triangle shape. Roll out evenly to required thickness, keeping a triangular shape.

Lightly grease a griddle or heavy-based frying pan with a little oil and place over a moderate heat.

Add the rolled paratha and cook until lightly coloured both sides, remove and keep warm and continue with the remaining dough. Best served warm, but can also be served cold.

alu paratha *(potato filled pastry)* Serves 4-6

500g plain flour
Pinch salt
150g butter, softened
200ml water, approximately
200g potatoes
30ml oil
Pinch panch porang seeds
20g onions, finely chopped
1tsp ginger and garlic paste (see page 21)
$^1/_2$tsp turmeric
1 fresh red chilli, finely shredded
1tsp garam masala
1tbsp freshly chopped coriander
Juice $^1/_2$ lemon
50ml olive oil

Sift together the flour and salt in a bowl, add butter and rub it between the fingers to a sandy texture. Make a well in the centre, add the water and mix to a soft dough.

Knead the dough on a lightly floured surface for few minutes, cover and let and allow to rest for at least half an hour.

Wash, peel, rewash and cut the potatoes into even sizes and boil in cold salted water until cooked. Drain and let dry thoroughly for 2-3 minutes over a very low heat. Mash the potatoes and set aside.

Heat the oil in a pan; fry the panch porang lightly until the flavour comes out, add onions, ginger/ garlic, turmeric, chilli, garam masala, mashed potato, salt and mix well.

Remove from the heat, add chopped coriander and lemon juice and allow to cool.

Divide the dough into 60g pieces. Roll out each piece of dough into a 14cm circle on a greased surface, add 2 tablespoons of mixture in the centre and spread evenly. Roll it tightly by pulling with your hand (like a Swiss roll) and brush with oil, make a round circle by bringing together fairly tightly from one end to finish like a round circled dough. Slightly flatten and roll out into round flat bread.

Shallow fry both sides to a light golden colour and serve warm.

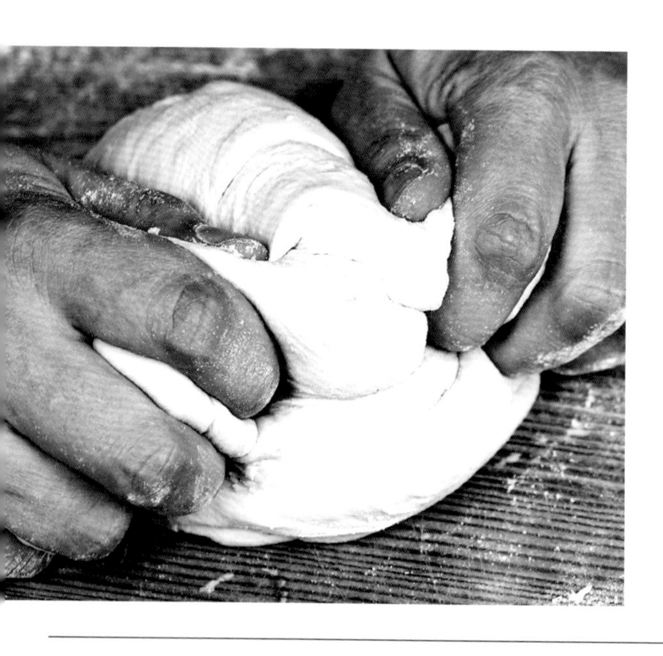

ting momo bread *(steamed buns)* (Serves 4-6)

500g plain flour
$^{1}/_{2}$tsp baking powder
Pinch salt
50g butter or margarine, cubed
10g granulated sugar
10g fresh yeast
320ml water
20ml olive oil

Sieve the flour, baking powder and salt into a bowl then add the butter or margarine and rub it in the flour. Make a well in the centre, add sugar and yeast.

Warm the water to body temperature and pour it to the well, cover with little flour from the sides and let it ferment for 3 minutes.

Shake the bowl and let the flour absorb the liquid, ensuring that the mixture of flour and water is soft and slightly sticky (a little bit of extra water may be required to get a good dough consistency).

Transfer onto a floured surface and knead for about 5 minutes, or until the right consistency of dough is achieved (soft). If the dough is wet, add a little extra flour in the kneading process.

Allow to prove in a warm place, covered with a damp cloth until it doubles in size, knock back to release the air, roll out the dough into a rectangular shape roughly 27cm by 35cm and to about 1.25cm thickness. Brush with oil and roll up lengthwise, brush again and cut into 12 even pieces.

Grease the steamer tray and arrange the dough, cut side facing upwards, steam for 10-12 minutes. Remove and serve hot.

'a very popular pastry dish known as ting momo in Tibetan and tee momo in Sherpa or Nepalese cuisine, it's served as an accompaniment to soup, vegetables and curry'

10

desserts

Desserts in Nepalese cuisine are enjoyed after the main meal. If the main meal is heavy and spicy, it is much preferred to make the dessert simple and well balanced.

Nepalese desserts are very similar to Indian desserts and are predominantly offered on special occasions or religious festivals

kheer *(rice pudding)* Serves 4 -6

100g short grain rice
100g granulated sugar
1 small cinnamon stick
5 cloves
1l fresh milk
20g butter
1tsp ground cardamom
40g sultana or raisins
20g flaked almonds, chopped

to garnish
Lightly toasted almonds

Pick and wash the rice, drain and put into a thick base saucepan. Add sugar, cinnamon, cloves and milk. Bring to the boil, reduce heat, add the butter and simmer for about 30-40 minutes, stirring occasionally to stop the mixture sticking to the bottom of the pan.

Remove and discard the cinnamon and cloves, stir in the cardamom powder, add sultanas or raisins and almonds and simmer another 10-15 minutes.

Check for texture and consistency which should be soft and moist and if required add some more boiled milk to adjust the consistency.

Pour into a suitable serving dish and serve.

'rice pudding with cinnamon and cardamon – the ultimate warming treat'

gajar ko haluwa *(sweet carrot pudding)*

Serves 4-6

200g carrots
600ml milk
60g white sugar
50g ground almonds
1/2tsp cardamom powder
50ml single cream

to serve
1/2 tbsp flaked almonds

Peel and coarsely grate the carrots, put into a saucepan and add milk, sugar and bring to the boil.

Stir occasionally, until the mixture is reduced to half. Using a hand blender, give a quick blend (about 8 seconds).

Mix in the ground almonds and cardamom powder and simmer gently for a few minutes.

Remove from heat, add the cream, mix well and serve.

alhaichi *(cardamom)* kulfee with raspberry coulis Serves 8-10

10 cardamom pods
2 x 410ml tins evaporated milk
100g light golden sugar
20ml gelatine, melted
50g pistachio nuts, roasted
150g mango, finely diced
2 x 284ml cartons single cream
50g dark chocolate
125ml double cream

to serve
Fresh strawberries and mango, raspberry coulis

to garnish
Crushed pistachio nuts

Crush the cardamom pods, remove the husk and grind the seeds to a fine powder. Boil the milk and sugar with the cardamom powder in a pan and let it simmer for 10 minutes, stirring occasionally. Remove from heat and allow to cool.

to prepare the gelatine

Soak in cold water until very soft, squeeze out the moisture and melt completely over warm water; for powder jelly: first dilute in a little cold milk and then pour over the boiled milk.

Add the gelatine to the milk mixture and whisk slowly, roughly crush the roasted pistachio nuts and mix with the milk. Add diced mango.

Semi whip the cream and combine all ingredients then pour into small ramekin dishes or small moulds, cover with cling film and put in freezer to set.

OR

Put the mixture into an ice-cream machine and mix until the mixture is completely set. Transfer into a clean container or into prepared rings and freeze.

to serve

Remove from freezer and allow to stand in the fridge for approximately 1 hour. Arrange the fruits and the kulfee, and serve garnished with some crushed pistachio nuts and raspberry coulis.

raspberry coulis

50g caster sugar
200g raspberries
2tbsp honey
Juice of 1/2 lemon
1/4tsp cardamom powder

Combine all ingredients in a small, deep bowl or plastic jug and blend for few seconds to a fine paste. Strain through the sieve and pour into a squeezy bottle. Serve as required to accompany the kulfee.

11

beverages

Tea is an important beverage for most people, especially in Nepal. Darjeeling tea, from the Himalayan foothills of Darjeeling is a world famous tea, known in the West as the champagne of tea. It has a unique flavour which requires careful brewing in order not to result in a bitter taste.

Tea is also of great importance in the Himalayan region where tea – known as chiya – is served throughout the day and friends and families are always offered chiya when they meet. Spicy tea is special chiya in most tea houses and the process of brewing spicy tea involves boiling sugar with spices added for flavour as well as acting as a medicinal deterrent against potential gum disease

Darjeeling tea 4 cups

600ml water
2tbsp Darjeeling tea, loose
100ml milk
2tbsp sugar (optional)

Boil the water (once only), add the Darjeeling tea, cover with lid and let it infuse for approximately 1-2 minutes.

Strain and pour into the cups, add a touch of warm milk and sugar and serve.

note

Adding too much milk may affect the flavour of the tea.

---

spicy milky tea 4 -6 cups

500ml water
250ml milk
6-8 tsp sugar
Seeds of 4 green cardamom pods
1 small piece cinnamon stick
10g root ginger peeled and sliced
4tsp loose tea or 4 teabags (preferably Nepalese)

Boil the water, milk and sugar with all the spices. Once boiled, remove from the heat, add the tea, cover and allow to infuse for 1 minute.

Strain and serve.

note

Do not re-boil the tea once the tea leaves or teabags are added.

12

puddings with nicci gurr

I'm a traditional British chef, and so it was thrilling to be invited to add a 'UK twist' to The Ultimate Nepalese Cook Book. What a wonderful way to celebrate tradition and bring together two cultures and their respective cuisines from the beautiful tea of the Nepalese Himalayas to the traditional Nepalese momos, all fused with a little bit of local English flavour.

What better way to round off a traditional Nepalese dinner than with a Nepalese inspired pudding?

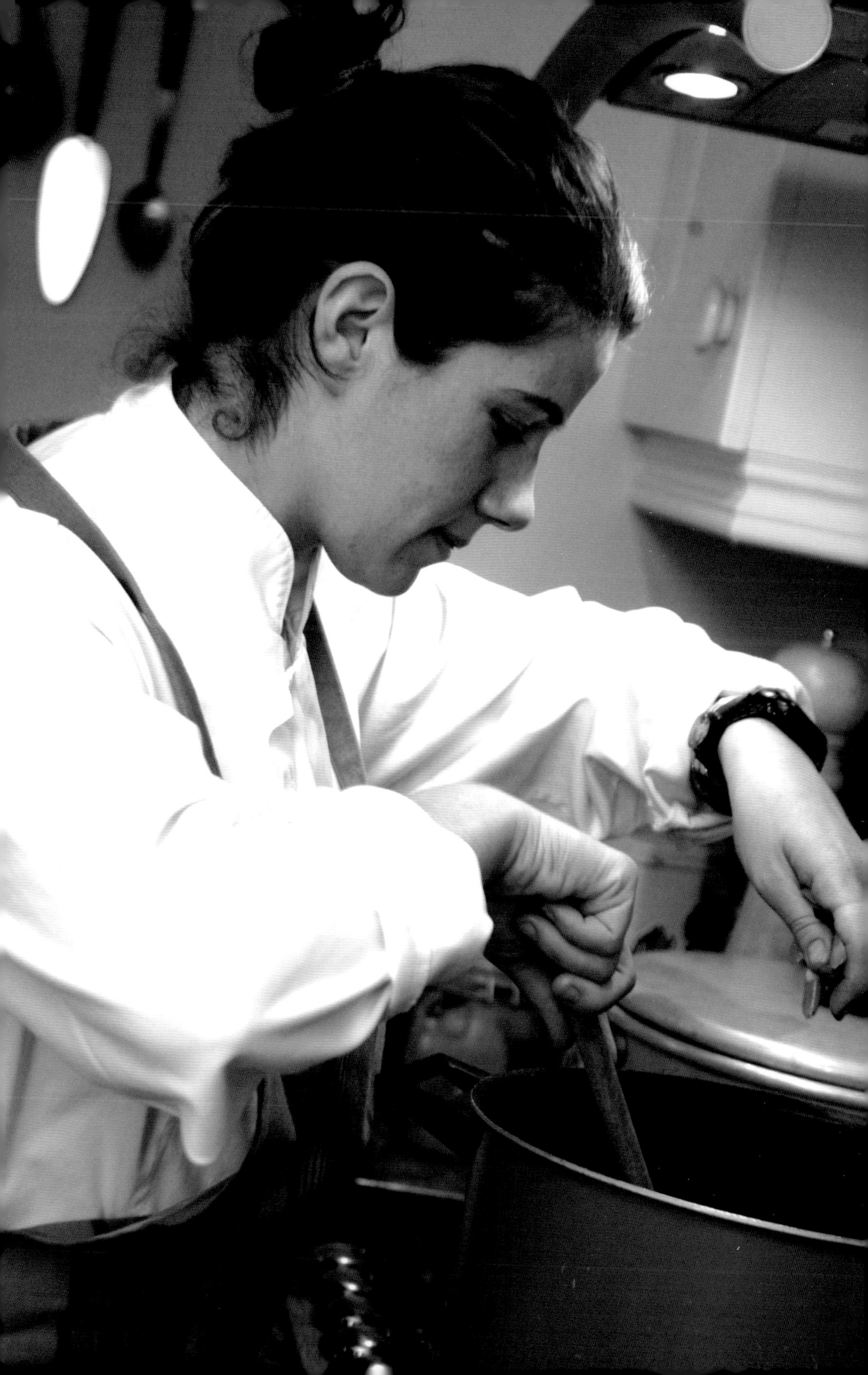

'I love this recipe; it is two Nepalese
recipes in one with a hidden treat'

momo pot stickers with chocolate & chilli

for the casing
275g plain flour
250ml – 300ml warm water
25g cocoa

for the khir (himalayan rice pudding)
25g butter
100g basmati rice
1 – 2 red chillies, deseeded
500ml pint whole milk
1/4 tbsp milk powder
50g sugar
100g dark chocolate
Plus extra chocolate for drizzling

for the casing

Mix flour, water and cocoa together to make a firm dough, cling film and rest for an hour.

In the mean time, make the kheer filling. In a large cooking pan, heat the butter over a low heat. Add rice and deseeded chillies and stir for 2-3 minutes. Pour milk into the rice mixture.

Add milk powder and sugar; stir thoroughly.

Bring to a boil and allow to simmer over a low heat, stirring constantly for about 20 minutes, or until the rice has softened. Take off the heat, drain any excess liquor, stir in the chocolate well. Set aside.

to cook

Bring a pan of water to a rolling boil or use a steamer with the grill well oiled.

Roll out a ball of dough and cut into a round using a cutter.

Place a small amount of filling in the centre of each pot sticker casing. Brush some water or excess liquor around the edges and fold in half. Press the edges with your fingers to seal.

Place the pot stickers in gently boiling water and cook until they float.

Remove and drain on paper towels. To serve, place the pot stickers on a plate, and drizzle some melted chocolate on top.

tea smoked mango cake

This cake is certainly one to impress! If you don't want to send smoke signals to your neighbours you can use the mango unsmoked – it still tastes great!

150g brown rice
150g dark brown sugar
60g leaf tea (Nepalese if possible)
1 whole ripe mango, which makes about 300g, skinned

for the cake
225g butter, softened, plus extra for greasing
225g caster sugar,
4 medium eggs
225g self-raising flour
2tsp baking powder
25g ground almonds

Mix the rice, sugar and tea leaves together and scatter into the bottom of a smoking pan.

Alternatively, line the base of a lidded pan with a double layer of aluminium foil and put the rice mix on top, then put another layer of foil on top of the rice mix and punch holes in it.

Cover with a lid and set over a medium heat for about 5-10 minutes, or until the mixture begins to smoke (CAUTION: this will generate a lot of smoke so keep the area well-ventilated by opening the doors and windows where possible).

Place the mango on the foil with the holes in and cover with foil and the lid. Lower the heat and smoke for 5 minutes, or until the mango has taken on the taste of the tea (you can tell by the smell), the mango will probably still be cool to touch. Turn off the heat and set aside.

Preheat the oven to 180°C/Fan160°C. Grease a deep 23-24cm spring form cake tin and line with baking paper. Cut the mango into 1cm pieces.

Using an electric hand whisk, cream together the butter and caster sugar in a bowl until pale and fluffy. Beat in the eggs, one at a time, adding a little flour with each addition to keep the mixture smooth and then add the mango pieces.

Sift the remaining flour and the baking powder into the bowl and fold in with the ground almonds.

Spoon into the prepared cake tin, lightly level the top. Bake in the oven for 1 hour or until well-risen, brown and a skewer inserted into the centre of the cake comes out clean. If the cake starts to look a little too brown, cover with a sheet of baking paper after about 45 minutes.

Leave to cool in the tin for 10 minutes. Remove the cake from the tin and place on a serving plate.

Cut the cake into generous wedges and serve warm with a spoonful of crème fraîche or Greek yogurt.

rice pudding with coconut and fennel

This classic comfort favourite is taken to another level with the addition of luxurious coconut and warming yet cleansing fennel seed.

60g pudding rice
80g caster sugar
1tsp fennel seeds
800ml – 1l milk
1 x 400ml tin coconut milk

to garnish
2-3tbsp desiccated or shaved coconut

Put the rice, sugar, crushed fennel seeds, and two-thirds of the milk, and all of the coconut milk in a thick-bottomed saucepan, bring to the boil and then place in an earthenware dish in the oven for about 40-45 minutes at 180°C.

Add more milk if the rice is getting dry, and cook until the rice is tender and a nice skin has formed on the top.

Garnish with extra toasted desiccated coconut.

---

tea loaf infused with sweet carrot and ginger

75g raisins
75g sultanas
75g currants
300ml tepid tea
200g young carrot, grated
200g soft light brown sugar
40g crystallised ginger
1 free-range egg, beaten
1tsp ground cinnamon
1tsp freshly grated nutmeg
1tsp ground ginger
250g self-raising flour
Butter, for greasing

Place the dried fruit and tea into a large bowl. Cover the bowl with a clean cloth and leave to soak overnight.

The next day, preheat the oven to 175°C.

Put carrot and sugar in a pan and heat until the sugar has dissolved and started to caramelize, then add the ginger, beaten egg and spices, and mix well. Mix with the soaked fruit and tea and then fold in the flour. Mix well.

Grease a 22cm x 10cm loaf tin. Spoon the mixture into the tin.

Transfer to the oven and bake for 1 1/4 hours, or until a skewer inserted into the cake comes out clean.

Serve slices of the tea loaf spread with unsalted butter.

'with the addition of ginger and sweet caramelised carrot, this quick tea loaf really is a cupboard staple'

green tea ice cream

An absolute classic dish, but this one doesn't need an ice cream machine. Rather oddly, this comes out a lovely pink colour, but to make the ice cream really green, add a teaspoon of Matcha powder which is Japanese green tea.

5 egg yolks
4tbsp sugar
4tbsp green tea (Nepalese if possible)
100ml freshly boiled water
400ml milk, scalded
1tsp Matcha powder (optional)

Lightly whisk the yolks, add sugar to the yolks and mix well. Mix the green tea with 100ml of freshly boiled water, strain and add to the milk, scald the milk and tea mixture over a low heat then, constantly stirring, add the scalded milk and tea mixture to the yolk mixture.

Return to the heat when the mixture has thickened and if using Matcha powder, stir in now. Stand in ice water to cool quickly, then pass through a sieve.

Transfer to a freezer-proof container and freeze for 2 hours, then mash the crystals with a fork.

Return to the freezer for a further 2 hours, mash again, and then allow to solidify.

Alternatively you can just mash once and set it in a terrine mould which has been lined with greaseproof paper for easy turning out, then slice.

pumpkin and tea pie

This is a real seasonal favourite and the addition of tea lightens up a heavy pudding, whilst giving it a little twist.

pastry

100g brown flour
100g white flour
100g butter
Water to bind

pumpkin mix

850g pumpkin or butternut squash should make 500g mashed cooked pumpkin or butternut squash
500ml black tea (Nepalese if possible)
350ml double cream
1tsp ground cinnamon
pinch ground cloves
1tsp ground mixed spice
1/2tsp ground ginger
1/2 tsp salt
1/2 tsp vanilla extract
150g brown sugar
6 medium eggs
1/2tsp salt

pecan topping

75g chopped pecans
50g butter
50g brown sugar

I always use half wholemeal flour and half white. The white lightens up the pastry while good wholemeal flour adds a distinct 'nutty' flavour. If using a porcelain dish then you must blind bake.

Blind baking is when you bake the pastry without the filling. You might do this if your pastry has a longer baking time or if you have a fairly wet filling that might soak into the pastry too much. If you are using an aluminium baking tin then there is no need to blind bake just slow down your oven to 150°C and extend your cooking time.

Sift the flour into a bowl, rub butter into the flour to form bread crumbs and then mix in cold water with a knife to form a dough that just holds together. Let the dough rest for 20 minutes.

Roll out and blind bake if necessary. Place greaseproof paper and baking beans or raw kidney beans inside the dish. This will put a light weight on the pastry to help prevent the pastry from shrinking away from the sides and keeping its shape while baking. Bake for 20 minutes at 180°C.

Peel and chop your pumpkin or large butternut squash, then place in a pan with some freshly made tea, simmer until cooked, drain, mash and cool.

Boil the cream and reduce until sticky, add spices, vanilla, sugar and eggs and mix together until smooth, then pour into a 22.5cm deep pastry base, and bake in a medium oven (about 180°C) for about 45 minutes to an hour.

to make topping

While the pie is baking, chop the pecans and add them to a saucepan with the butter and brown sugar. Over a low to medium heat let the butter sizzle and caramelize the sugar. Remove from heat.

Set aside until the pie has cooked for about 45 minutes to 1 hour and has firmed up a bit and just looks soft or wet in the centre. Then remove pie from oven and sprinkle the pecan topping evenly all over the top of the pie.

milk balls with salty tea pistachio

This is a Nepalese classic, and absolutely delicious.

1800ml milk
2tbsp black tea leaves (Nepalese if possible)
50g butter
1 -2 chillis, deseeded
Pinch of salt
1tsp black cardamoms, crushed
175g castor sugar
165g cottage cheese
115g plain flour
1tsp orange flower water

to garnish
Pistachio nuts

Put the milk, tea and butter, chillis and salt into a large pan. Bring to the boil, infuse and strain.

Add the crushed cardamoms to the pan.

Simmer the mixture over a medium heat until it has been reduced by half and thickened slightly, then add the sugar.

Turn the heat down as low as possible under the pan.

Beat the cottage cheese and flour together, divide into six or eight portions and roll these into balls.

Flatten each one slightly and drop them into the pan of milk mixture.

Simmer for 10-15 minutes. Remove the pan from the heat and carefully transfer the balls into a serving bowl.

Cool completely, and then stir the orange flower water into the milk mixture, and pour over the balls.

Just before serving, chop the pistachio nuts and sprinkle over the top.

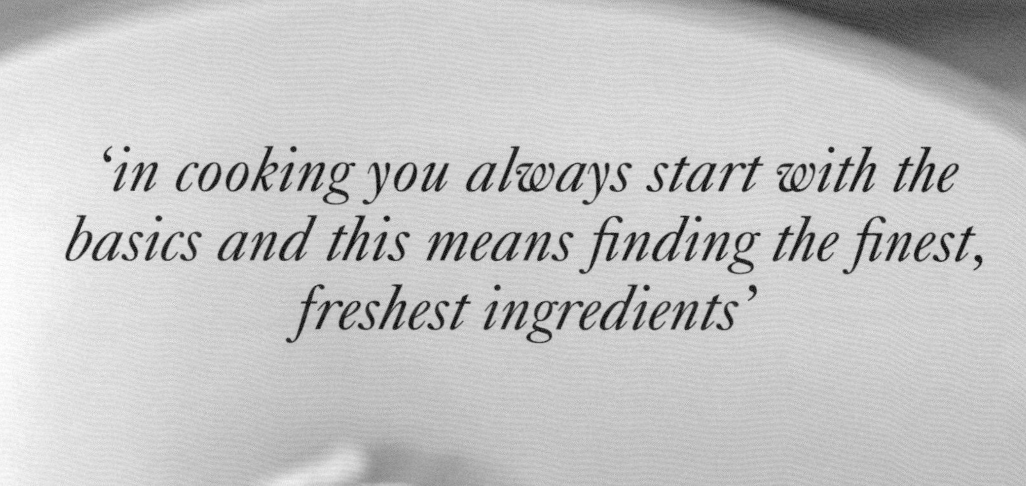

'in cooking you always start with the basics and this means finding the finest, freshest ingredients'

green tea rice balls with banana

This recipe can be a bit fiddly but is really worth a go and when you bite into the ball the banana is a lovely surprise!

2tbsp green tea (Nepalese if possible)
400g coconut milk
150g banana (about 2 bananas)
1tsp cinnamon
300g rice flour
$^{1}/_{2}$tsp oil
60g dried shredded coconut (toasted)

Add the tea and coconut milk to a pan and heat through, then stand to allow the tea to infuse; strain, and cool. While cooling, mash the banana with the cinnamon and refrigerate.

Stir the coconut milk and tea mixture slowly into the flour to form a dough, similar to play dough!

You may need to add slightly more coconut milk, or more flour depending on how thin your coconut milk is. The dough should be quite stiff and shouldn't stick to your hands (if it does, it requires a little more flour). If it doesn't stick together it's too dry – add a little more coconut milk.

Take a little of the dough in your hands and form a ball. Now indent the sticky rice ball and place about 1tsp of the cold banana mix in the rice ball. Pinch the sides to cover the banana and close it. Your first attempts will probably look awful, but persevere and find your own way!

Try flattening some of the dough and placing some of the banana mix in the middle, then almost mould a sphere around it.

Gently roll it again to return it to a ball shape. Place on a plate dusted with rice flour.

Bring some water to a rolling boil; drop the rice balls into the pot. They will sink to the bottom at first, and then rise to the surface. Once the balls have risen to the surface, continue cooking for 2 more minutes, on a reduced heat.

Once cooked, use a small strainer to remove the rice balls from the water and place in an oiled bowl.

Place the dried shredded coconut in a bowl and roll the sticky rice balls in the coconut to coat.

Place the finished rice balls on a plate, and serve.

treacle tart with black salt

This is a lovely flavoured tart – the salt really opens up the flavours of the treacle.

100g brown flour
100g white flour
100g butter
Cold water to bind

for the filling
60g breadcrumbs
Pinch of black salt
4tbsp Golden Syrup

Sift the flour into a bowl, rub the butter into the flour to form bread crumbs, and then mix in cold water with a knife to form a dough that just holds together. Let the dough rest for 20 minutes.

Roll out and blind bake if needed (see page 145).

to make filling
Prepare the tart filling by putting the breadcrumbs and salt in a saucepan, add the Golden Syrup and stir over heat until the mixture is smooth.

Pour the Golden Syrup mix into the tart base and place in the oven at 200°C for 20 minutes and then 180°C for 10 minutes. Then take out of the oven and cool on a rack. Eat when it has cooled partially or completely. It will keep for up to 3 days in a cake tin in the fridge.

glossary

ENGLISH	GURKHALI	ENGLISH	GURKHALI
Asparagus	Kurilo	Lovage or Ajowan	Jwano
Aubergine	Bhenta/Baighun	Mace	Jaipatri
Bamboo Shoots	Tama	Millet	Kodo
Bay Leaf	Tej Paat	Mushroom	Chyau
Beetroot	Chukander	Mustard (Green)	Tori Ko Saag
Black Cumin	Kalo Jira/Mungrelo	Mustard Seeds (Dark)	Rayo/Tori
Black-Eyed Peas	Maas or Kalo Dahl	Mustard Seeds (Yellow)	Sarsyun
Buckwheat	Phapar	Nutmeg	Jaiphal
Cabbage	Banda Kopi	Oats	Jau
Cardamom (Black)	Alaichi	Oil	Tel
Cardamom (Green)	Sukmel	Okra	Chiple Bhendi
Carrot	Gajar	Peas (Green)	Kerao Matar
Cashew Nuts	Kaju	Pepper (Ground)	Dhulo Marich
Cauliflower	Phulkopi	Pepper (Bell)	Bhede Khursani
Chickpea	Chana Dahl	Pepper (Black)	Kalo Marich
Gram Flour	Besan	Potato	Ahaloo
Chilli	Khursani	Pumpkin	Pharsi
Chive	Chhyapi	Rice	Chamal
Chive (Chinese)	Dundu Ko Saag	Saffron	Kesar
Cinnamon	Dalchini	Salt	Noon
Clove	Lwang	Semolina	Suji
Coconut	Nariwal	Sesame Seeds	Til Ko Dana
Coriander	Dhaniya	Soya Beans	Bhatmas
Corn	Makai	Spinach	Palungo/Saag
Cucumber	Kankra	Split Peas	Kerao Ko Dana
Cumin	Jira	Spring Onions	Pyaj Ko Saag
Fennel Seeds	Saunf	Spice	Masala
Fenugreek	Methi	Spices (Mixed Seeds)	Panch Porang
Flour	Pitho	Sweet Potato	Sakarkhanda
Fresh Coriander	Hario Dhaniya	Tamarind	Titiri
Garlic	Lasun	Taro or Eddo	Pindalu
Ginger	Aduwa	Tea	Chiya
Green Beans	Seebhi	Tomato	Golbheda
Green Dill	Saunf Ko Saag	Turmeric	Besar
Jaggery	Misri	Vinegar	Sirkaa
Lentils	Musuri Dahl	Yam	Tarul
Himalayan Pepper	Timmur	Yogurt	Dahi

index